Beneath This Thick Skin

A collection of short stories

by

Nyasha Melissa Chiyanike

First published in Great Britain in 2024 by:

Carnelian Heart Publishing Ltd
Suite A
82 James Carter Road
Mildenhall
Suffolk
IP28 7DE
UK

www.carnelianheartpublishing.co.uk

Paperback ISBN   978-1-914287-53-4
Hardback ISBN   978-1-914287-54-1

A CIP catalogue record for this book is available from the British Library.

This collection of short stories is entirely a work of fiction. The names, characters and incidents portrayed in it are the work of the author's imagination. Any resemblance to actual persons, living or dead, is purely coincidental.

Editors:

Panashe Lazarus Nyagwambo & Memory Chirere

Cover Art: Kirk Chai

Cover Layout: Rebeca Covers

Typeset by Carnelian Heart Publishing Ltd

Layout and formatting by DanTs Media

To my friends and family; you have been my pillars of support throughout this writing journey. I love and appreciate you.

Contents

"The most powerful battles are the ones we fight in silence"
– Unknown

Zadziso

I had just come back from the well when I first noticed something was off. Amai was not waiting in the kitchen to help me take down the twenty-litre bucket from my head. A hushed silence fell over the entire household. I leaned against the wall for balance as I took down the bucket. I shrugged at the sound of water hitting the floor as about a quarter of the contents spilled over. I placed the bucket on the built-in earthen bench in the kitchen, then walked out to grab the old cotton t-shirt we used as a mop.

"Nyarai! Thank goodness you're back." It was Ma Ziviro who spoke anxiously as she approached our compound. She was sweaty and breathless.

"Is it Amai? Where is she? Did something happen to her?"

"No, my dear. Your mother is ok, just a little worried. Zadziso still hasn't returned from school."

I let out a sigh of relief.

"Have you seen him anywhere?" she asked.

"No. Zadziso is such a little rascal," I scoffed. "He is probably somewhere along the way playing with his friends."

"Your mother has gone to check if his friends are home yet. Do call me when she gets back."

"It's alright Ma. Thank you for your concern," I said, before walking back into the kitchen.

As soon as I was done mopping up, I headed out and picked some dry twigs so I could make a fire. I arranged them and the firewood in a circle at the centre of the kitchen. The fireplace was a concave circular depression on the black floor with three boulders placed at the edges to make a sort of tripod to support the pots. I pulled a few strands of grass from the edge of the thatched roof and added them to the pile before lighting a matchstick. Amai had always reprimanded me for doing that. She said it weakened the roof, but I still did it when she was not around.

After the fire was set, I placed a clay pot of beans onto it then stood by the doorstep looking for Amai. I watched as the sun slowly crawled into the horizon, casting its reddish beams over the compound. I could feel myself getting unsettled with each passing minute. I was more annoyed than nervous.

This was not the first time Zadziso had been out late. The other time he had walked for kilometres with his friends, Teurai and Mukundi to collect *mazhanje* from the forests around Zindoga. We had all been worried sick and at dusk, Baba had gathered a search team to go look for them. They were spotted on their way back home and Baba beat the three boys up. He forbade Zadziso from playing with Teurai and Mukundi. Zadziso quickly found his way into another clique. I wondered what he was up to this time. I had always complained that he was a spoiled brat. A month would not pass without him cooking up some mischief that got everyone stressed.

After a couple of minutes, Amai returned with a sullen look on her face. "His friends are at home. They said he was still writing his corrections when they left," she spoke with a voice audibly filled with terror.

"Don't worry Amai. He is probably out there somewhere doing something silly. You know how Zadziso is," I said.

"I don't know, my daughter. I have a very bad feeling about this. Is your father back yet?"

I shook my head.

"Ma Ziviro came looking for you. She instructed me to call her as soon as you came back," I added more wood to the fire.

"You can go call her."

I rushed out of the kitchen towards the Ziviro homestead. They were as worried as Amai. Having no sons of their own, Zadziso always helped herd their goats and cattle. I was tempted to unpack my thoughts on how Zadziso was just a delinquent attention seeker, but I bit my tongue. Ma Ziviro held my hand as we walked back home. The sun had finally rested beyond the hills, leaving the village in twilight darkness. I hummed a song to try and dilute the tension that clothed us.

As we approached Amai's hut, I saw Baba staggering in. He had a bottle clutched in his hand and I instantly knew things were about to be ugly. I stayed behind Ma Ziviro as we walked into the kitchen, clutching her arm.

Baba's voice was erupting.

"What do you mean he is not back yet? Is he now the father of the house?"

"Manheru," Ma Ziviro greeted calmly as she went to sit next to Amai on the reed mat. I followed suit.

Baba sighed exasperatedly then threw his bottle down. We recoiled and looked away as the bottle shattered and showers of beer rained on us.

"I have no rest in this house," he muttered as he walked towards the door. "Stay here. I will gather some people to help look for the boy. When I find him, I swear I am going to beat the life out of him."

Amai rubbed her eyes, trying to hide her tears. Baba was an occasional drinker but those few times he took to beer, he would cover up for all the days of sobriety. The fire was slowly dying out, casting eerie shadows on the walls. I moved closer and blew into the fire until bright yellow flames grew and began to dance in the fireplace. I busied myself with preparing supper while Amai conversed with Ma Ziviro. When the food was ready, neither of us was able to eat and we moved outside in anticipation of seeing Zadziso arrive.

Around midnight, Baba returned with the other men of the village. He was still agitated. They had searched in all the neighbouring villages and gone back to the school, but no one had seen Zadziso.

"Tomorrow morning we will go into the woods and search. All the men and young boys of the village will set out before the break of day," Mr Ziviro addressed the small crowd. Baba disappeared into his bedroom without a single word. The gathering dissipated to their respective homesteads. Amai walked back to the kitchen. There was no way she could spend the night with Baba. I knew she would not be able to sleep so I joined her in silence.

As soon as the darkness of the night began to fade, Baba walked out of his room and the other men of the village converged at our compound. As soon as I heard voices building up outside, I walked out with ears open wider than my eyes. I did not want to miss any details about what would happen next. Amai genuflected as she greeted Baba, but he did not respond. He was usually poetic about his morning greetings but on this particular morning, his vibrance was gone.

"Did you manage to get some sleep?" Amai went at it again.

"Woman! Stop asking silly questions. Let me speak to the other men and see how best we can clean up your mess."

"Go fetch water from the well," Amai whispered to me.

"But I fetched water in the eveni…" the look that Amai gave me shut me up. I grabbed a bucket and begrudgingly walked to the well. I hated it when I was chased away when important matters were being discussed.

The men planned how they would move out as teams. Baba would go to the police while everyone else went into the woods and other villages. As I walked away, the voices from our compound slowly faded. All I could hear were hushed murmurs. There was a combination of panic, fear and desperation.

The well was not my favourite place in the morning. The grass around was always covered in frost and it made my legs itchy. The upside though was that the water was always cleaner that time of day. I stretched my back before pulling away the metal lid that covered the well. Its metallic clang echoed inside as it fell on the other side. I grabbed the small bucket strapped to a rope that we used to draw the water. Amai had taught me to throw it in upside down so I could fill up my bucket faster. I peered into the well before throwing in the little bucket and my heart thumped. A piercing scream involuntarily escaped my mouth and I felt chills creeping all over my body. I regressed to lean on a nearby tree.

***

Amai reached the well at full speed and likewise wailed hysterically. Had it not been for Mr Ziviro who followed right behind her, she would have jumped right in.

"Oh Christ," the other villagers mumbled as they each looked into the well and walked past, shaking their heads.

I fell right into Amai's arms and cried out in disbelief. A crowd slowly grew and Mr Ziviro ordered people to keep their distance from the well. He went to a nearby tree and drew some bark which he threaded together. One of the young men of the village climbed down the well. He was in there for a long time before he emerged with Zadziso's mottled body strapped to his back with the threaded bark. At the sight of the lifeless body, our wailing amplified, echoed by that of the onlookers.

As his naked body was laid on the ground, I noticed the cut on his neck and my heart sank. What kind of an animal would do that to an eleven-year-old? I also saw that his penis was missing but the site was quickly covered up with leaves. The thought of what had happened to my brother ate through me.

I then thought of Baba and my tears ceased. I wondered if he was also here and if he could see the atrocity of what had been done to his son. Slowly, I let go of Amai and looked around. Baba was standing still on the other side of the well. He did not flinch as the entire village fell into chaos. I hated that about him. He was always tough. I had watched him when Gogo Ngwaru had passed on and at his little brother's funeral. He had not shed a single tear. He was doing the same thing now and it disgusted me.

The police were called, and it took hours for them to show up. I could feel anger bubbling within me when they said the body should have been left untouched until they had arrived. How could we have left our Zadziso in that well for hours?

Zadziso's funeral would only be carried out after the completion of investigations. Our village had a strong cultural legislation that ruled nobody would be buried with missing parts, so I knew there was going to be a long stretch before Zadziso's burial.

I had often heard stories of ritualistic killings but never had I imagined such doom befalling my own family. Selfish people in search of riches would kill young children and harvest blood and private parts. They would take these to specialists and perform rituals that were believed to summon wealth.

Almost everyone in the village was a suspect. It was difficult even for the police to decipher where exactly to start. Days passed by slowly and still nothing tangible had come out of the investigations. At home, Amai cried day in, day out. She became non-functional. She did not clean or cook and hardly spoke. Baba drank more beer than usual. He would walk to the police station each day to assess the progress of the case, and each day he would come back with a fresh dishing of disappointment.

The picture of Zadziso's body down that well did not leave my mind. It filled me with disgust and anger. I hated myself for having failed to protect my brother. I especially regretted having been the one to find him in that spot. I struggled to hold back my tears each day and I had to force myself to be the shoulder Amai needed to lean on. I took each day as it came, praying that one day I would be able to close my eyes and not have nightmares.

On a sad Thursday morning, as had become the norm, I woke up early to sweep the yard. I rushed through all my chores so I could get a little rest before heading to the forest to gather some firewood. As I moved out of the kitchen, holding a claypot so I could wash it outside, I was surprised to see two police officers approaching our compound. I greeted them and they requested for my parents.

"Go inside," Amai commanded me when they came out. I stood by the window following the conversation.

"We found a suspect," one of the policemen spoke. "A farmworker from the next village was found with a bloody knife. We brought him in for questioning. He confessed to having played a role in the killing of your son." The police officer paused and looked at Baba. "His story leads back to you. We have to take you in for questioning."

"Have you no shame," Amai interjected. "The man just lost his son. Show some empathy."

"We are just doing our job, Ma," he replied as he cuffed Baba.

"Are the handcuffs really necessary?" she spoke through tears. "Let him go, you heartless creatures."

"Calm down my wife. I will be back soon," Baba said gently.

I rushed out in tears and hugged Amai.

"It never rains but it pours, my daughter," she cried out.

A few neighbours walked towards our homestead and watched as Baba was frogmarched away. They shook their heads, unable to fashion their thoughts into words. I could tell that they pitied us.

As soon as Baba and the policemen disappeared into the distance, Amai walked to their bedroom. She kept muttering words I could not understand. I feared the pressure was getting to her head and she could end up like Ma Jocie whom everyone said was crazy. I followed her and stood at the door in silence.

Amai took down a box from the dressing table and threw the contents onto the bed. She ran her hands through the pile aggressively then grabbed a picture. She stared at it for seconds before breaking into tears. It was a picture of Zadziso and I next to a Christmas tree at church. It had been taken the previous year and I still recalled the day vividly.

She took down another box and emptied the contents and when she was done, she moved to the drawers. She picked out everything that reminded her of Zadziso and clasped it for minutes before moving to the next. After the drawers, she delved into the wardrobe until every piece of clothing was out before she moved to the old suitcases that were stacked in a corner. As she ruffled through the contents, she pulled out a shirt. It was the same shirt Baba had been wearing the day Zadziso had gone missing. She hugged the shirt and once again broke into tears.

The shirt was silky and the blue material glistened slightly from where Amai stood. It had patches of tiny leaves embroidered all over. Pieces of thread stuck out in different directions from overuse. The armpit areas had faded and I knew it would not be long before the stitches gave up. I had never really liked the shirt on Baba. I always felt like it was a little too feminine. As Amai put away the shirt, a peculiar stain caught her eye. The left sleeve had what looked vaguely like a washed-out blood stain. Amai turned and gave me a look.

Her eyes seemed to ask, "Do you see what I see?"

I did not know how to react.

A darker night

I plunged into the thick darkness and raced with the wind, its particles and dustiness vigorously whipping my face. I could barely feel my feet as they, in their nudity, pounded on what I assumed was the patchy tarred road that led home. The tension in my lips increased just outside the dry cave that was my mouth, but it was nothing compared to the war that ravaged my lungs. I continued to take desperate gasps of air, using the pain that accompanied each breath as a diversion for the fear that loomed inside of me.

I heard another gunshot and more tears slipped from the edges of my eyes. Stopping was not an option.

As I turned into another dark alley, a piercing sensation ran from my right heel, up my spine and to my head, forcing me to a sudden, sharp stop. I bumped into a garbage can, and with a thud, embraced the rocky ground. Reflexively, my hands gripped my throbbing foot. I felt the grainy fluid that ran from the core of excruciating pain, a mixture of sand and blood. My fingers landed on a small piece of what I assumed was glass that was lodged in my heel. I pulled it out then tore a piece of my shirt and wrapped it around my foot. I ran my shaky hands over my skin in search of more wounds, anything serious, perhaps a gunshot. My search yielded no more than a heaving sigh of relief.

"You are okay. You are alive," I whispered to myself.

It was only then, as soon as I heard the words that I brooded over it: I was not ok, nothing was ok.

The night's silence was deafening, so profound I could almost hear the blood squeeze through my ventricles. The cold, still air of the trashed-up alley in which I sat huddled was a perfect complement to the coldness that had overtaken my soul. After hours of contemplation, I had come to terms with the fact that my life would never be the same after this night.

"Men are not punished *for* their sins but *by* them." Those were the words the old lady had whispered to me as her spirit evanesced from her body. Her sombre voice resonated in my head and sent an eruption of goosebumps all over my sweaty skin. Her bloody face was all my mind could picture. I wished she knew, wherever she was, that I was no killer, that what had happened to her was only an unfortunate accident. I hoped she understood we had both fallen victim to the heat of the moment.

I rested my chin onto my knees as I tried to gather tattered, half-formed bits of pieces of prayers I had heard people say for the deceased. The tears came again and I rolled in the dusty alley like a baby yearning for an embrace. Everything had happened so fast, an entire tragic life in the space of that one night.

I had made up my mind the previous day that I was done with my life of crime. My mother had begged me through tears to go back to being the person I had been before, an obedient boy who focussed only on school. On the same day, Thomas, our neighbour, had been arrested for selling marijuana from his little tuckshop. I had dealt with Thomas on many occasions and watching him being driven away in chains filled me with fear. My mother's cries were the final nail in the coffin, forcing me into contemplation.

It was then that it had struck me; the old me would have been disappointed with who I had turned out to be. I had given up everything I had worked so hard for over the past years. In a few months, I had stopped going to school and quit church. I impregnated two young girls in my neighbourhood and denied responsibility. Threats had been made to go for DNA tests, but I knew they could never afford them, so I simply moved on with my life, carefree. Worst of all, I got addicted to crystal meth and the other cheap drugs I sold, and I had found my way into a gang. I had narrowed my expectations from life so thinly that all I cared about was a quick high and temporary mania. It gave me consolation to know I was a failure and no one expected anything of me. I was living life on the line, but at least I had not given in to the societal standards of whom I was expected to be. However, in spite of this false positivity I pampered myself with, I knew deep down I wanted out.

At first, I had been comfortable with this life, which came with very little responsibility, but with time it had turned out to be a swim in a river. The current was gradually strengthening, and I was slowly losing it. I had moved from telling petty lies to torturing the vulnerable, and before I knew it, I was everything a younger me had feared.

Going back to who I had been before would not be easy. I had to start all over again. I was too far from where I had been, and I was not sure I knew how to go back. I had sunken deep and was so wrapped up in my corrupt ways. For my parents, however, I was willing to fight the battle back to being a decent son, one they could point to in public without shame. I would go with my gang on one last mission and that would be the end. All I needed was a little cash to sustain myself on a new leaf. I would have one last night of crime and by the break of dawn, I would be a brand-new creation.

On the special day that marked my resignation from the life of worthlessness, I spent hours with the gang planning out how we would strike a house in the suburbs.

"There is a safe in the bedroom where you will find at least five-thousand dollars. Leave nothing behind and kill anyone who stands in your way," Klaus, the gang leader instructed as he puffed on a joint. The pungent smoke swirled above us like some holy spirit, up to the mould infested ceiling of the small cabin. These words were an anthem; recited each day before we headed out for an assignment, "Kill anyone who stands in the way." All previous missions had, however, ended in threats. Just the sight of our guns would push our victims into submission. We were not killers; *I* was not a killer.

"Good luck," he gave me a pat on the back before we moved out for the hunt.

My gut churned as it always did on the other days when we set out. There was never any guarantee of safety, and yet we still showed up when duty called. In an hour, we had positioned ourselves in the shadows within the high walls of a compound in Acacia. As we had planned, Jabu, a gangly fella, crawled to the door and gave a knock before rushing back into hiding. The lights were on in minutes and seconds later, the door gaped.

"Who is it?" the old lady shouted, and I could sense the fear in her shrill voice. The silence that followed compelled the old lady further out of the house as she scanned the premises slowly. It took us moments to seize her and hijack the house before she could call for help.

Locating the safe was not a problem. It was an old, ashy box mounted just next to a coat hanger. The little box was locked.

"Where is the key?" The gang was gentle in their questioning at first. Giving away the keys would have made everything easier, but the old lady, perhaps in some warped sense of bravado or out of sheer stupidity, tried to fight. Any average person could easily tell that she was as harmless as a puppy, but we were not average people. The increasing violence of the team as they asked and searched for the keys did not reflect any of that understanding. Portraits were torn, mirrors broken and drawers emptied anxiously. In minutes, we were all busy searching for the keys, too busy to notice the old lady's hand slide up a wall and hit the emergency panic button. The blaring alarm brought everyone to a sudden halt. And then the winds went up.

"What have you done? What have you done?" Takudzwa, one of the older gang members charged at the old lady before landing a couple of slaps and heavy kicks on her wrinkled face. It was instantly a Picasso of blood.

"We need to get out of here quick. Shoot her!" Takudzwa gave me the order as the team got ready to leave.

"What are you waiting for?" Everyone was getting impatient.

My limbs jellied but I somehow gathered enough strength to pull out the pistol that was balanced on my waistline. I battled the tremor that had now invaded my entire system and aimed for her bloody forehead. My conscience weighed down on my arm like gravity and I could feel the energy fading from my limbs. I was caught between being a chicken or a killer. The fury of my team grew with each second that I hesitated. I closed my eyes and felt like a passenger in my own body as I felt the pressure of the trigger against my finger.

I did not watch her die, but I had heard her words as her life ebbed away.

We scattered frantically towards the gate where we were met by police officers with Rottweilers. They sprung out enthusiastically from the cars that, at the same moment, were pulling up at the scene. It was one man for himself.

Screams, gunshots, dogs barking, and flashing lights; everything was pointing to disaster and regret for the team. Chaos grabbed rule of the situation and all I could think of was running for my life. I watched as others ran, fell or were pulled into the police cars. The oversize sneakers I had stolen from my father slipped off my feet, but I kept going, an adrenaline fuelled frenzy into the dark of the night. I continued to run through bushes and empty streets until I found myself in a dirty alley, with a wounded heel and the waking nightmare of what had happened to keep me company.

Guilt would not let me close my eyes the entire night. The only cover I had to wrap myself in was the blanket of the icy darkness, the very thing that I had become. I could not stand being myself anymore. I rubbed my hands on my face and they disgusted me, the hands that could take an innocent life. An old lady had died and I was to blame. The last ride had turned out to be the worst. Some of my mates had died, some had been arrested, and soon, I would join either of them. I waited for the night to pass. Whatever would happen the next day, I was ready to face it.

The sun came out of hiding and everything came to life, but the darkness did not go away. It was only then that I realised I had spent the night with dead rats next to me and that I looked like the homeless men I often saw on the streets. I limped out of the alley and quickly found the path that led home. The brightness of the day was a direct contrast to the terror of the previous night. A cool breeze whistled through the leaves, creating a melody that resonated well with the sound of the birds that twittered in the distance as I slowly made my way home.

Echoes of the Gregorian chant from a nearby Roman Catholic Church floated towards my ears, bringing to me a calmness I had always yearned for. I had passed by this spot each day to earn myself a few seconds of feeling like I was less of a sinner. It always gave me consolation to get in touch with my peaceful side after each day of horrific acts. I looked up and admired the patches of clear blue sky that were partially masked by the umbrella-shaped Jacaranda trees that lined the path. Purple flowers impregnated the trees, creating a heavenly scene. I took a deep breath and the stench of rotting Jacaranda flowers ambushed my nostrils, demolishing the false peace I had built up in the moment. A frown of disgust settled on my face as I found my way back to the horrors of my life.

I paced up and turned into the street that led to our house. I could not wait to get home. Maybe Amai's smile would make me feel better, or perhaps Baba's comforting, calm words. I was going to apologise to Baba for failing to follow his good examples and to Amai for having thrown away each lesson she had taught me as I was growing up. Maybe we would all hold hands and pray as we had done in the good old days. Prayer had always been the answer to all our problems. I needed it now more than ever.

As I approached the doorstep, tears welled in my eyes. I could not think of where I would start with my story; how I would explain the blood on my shirt or where I had been the entire night or with whom. I did not deserve to be here. I did not deserve my loving parents. The hate I felt towards myself weighed down on me as I reached for the doorknob and twisted it. I plunged my torso right into the door, which swung open and smashed violently into the adjacent wall. I staggered to maintain my balance and leaned on the open doorway for a second. My eyes raced first to my mother who sat in tears in Baba's arms, his hand caressing her back, then to the two police officers who sat on the opposite couch. In that moment, I realised, with some relief, that I would not need to explain anything. I would neither run nor hide. I was a killer now, and I had to go down like one.

"I am sorry," was all I could say as the handcuffs clipped onto my wrists.

This is not goodbye

Her dazzling white dress hugged her body with breath robbing precision, showing off her hourglass make. Two vertical slits raced from her ankles to her thighs, revealing just enough of her chocolate brown skin to get him excited. Gatherings of sweat dotted her flawless skin, giving the impression of an ice-cold beer he desperately wanted to get a taste of. Her neck made a graceful turn and she flashed him a naughty smile and a wink.

"Catch me if you can," she teased as she picked a theatrical run along the picturesquely green lawn.

He abruptly stood from the small log on which he had been sitting and paced towards her, butterflies racing up from the ground like reverse rainfall in synchrony with the rhythm of their footsteps.

"Here comes the tickle monster!" his deep voice roared as he inched closer towards her. He wanted to hold her and tell her how much he loved her.

"Kuda!" she kept yelling his name between giggles. The giggles died down with each second and her tone grew angrier with each call. He reached out his hand when suddenly, a hard object landed on his forehead, setting his brains on a stir, excruciating pain radiating from the point.

"Kudakwashe! Kuda!"

He struggled to open his eyes and through his daze, spotted his mother pitched at the door, furiously calling out his name and ready to launch another shoe at him. "What has got into you boy? Get up and prepare for the service. You need to make a good impression today. We are already behind time." She was screaming the commands at him, sparing no time to so much as breathe. "I have put a bucket of warm water in the bathroom. It's a bit cold today," Mrs Dube went on with a tinge of remorse in her speech. "I have already bathed Nkosi and I will feed him while you bath."

Kuda nodded absently and dragged himself out of bed. He heard Nkosi's frail crying emanating from his mother's bedroom, the second of their three roomed house, and his heart sank. He felt his eyes watering and suddenly became aware of the way his head cracked. He had cried himself to sleep the previous night and now he was back to the reality he dreaded so much, the mess that was his life.

As soon as his mother left the room and shut the door behind her, Kuda went back to his bed, still fighting back tears. This was the sixth consecutive night he had dreamt of Tariro. He missed her so much, it was paralysing. Nothing was the same without her. Nkosi's very existence was a constant reminder of the intimate moments he had shared with her and his son's presence made everything so much harder. Deep down Kuda wished to be a good father but without a good mother by his side to help him raise his son, he felt he lacked the capacity to wear those shoes. He had even grown to slightly hate his own child, who was a living reminder of just how cruel life could be.

On particularly difficult days, Kuda had found solace in writing and today was the hardest he had to endure. He reached out for his diary and tore out a piece of paper then began to write.

Dear Tari

It is day seventy-four. I am still waiting for a call or a text from you. I check my phone every minute hoping to see that one notification that never comes. Everyone says I am crazy. They say

I should move on but that's something I will not do in this life or the next.

I am the only one who believes you are still out there somewhere, holding on to the love we shared and I know you will come back to me. I will never give up on our love. I pray for you each night. I pray for your health and safe return to us. I only wish the rest of the world understood just how much you mean to me; maybe then they would stop pestering me to give up.

It hurts me that you never said goodbye and I blame myself for not being around that day. Maybe I would have held your hand and convinced you to stay. I still vividly remember the disappointment that I got when I walked into our home and you were not there. I relive that feeling every single day. I do not hate you for leaving. I could never hate you.

I love you, just as much as I did right from the start. I still believe that you are the one for me and that is why I keep fighting, even when the whole world is against me. I will never stop fighting for our love.

I wish I knew where to address this letter because I know it probably hurts you to go this long without hearing from me.

I cannot wait for the day we will reunite. I will take you to that Italian restaurant you always wanted to try out. I will snap countless pictures of you and Nkosi. He misses you too. I am sure it's all he would ever speak of if he talked. He needs you. I cannot look at him with fatherly love without your motherly breath sweeping over my shoulder. I wish I had it in me to be there for him but I can't, not without you.

Come back baby. Come back to us.
Lots of love
Kuda

As soon as he was done writing, Kuda crumpled up the piece of paper and threw it under the bed where it joined the growing heap of unsent letters to Tariro.

"Hey *wena*, Kuda, go and bath!"

He gathered the little strength he had and dragged himself to the bathroom. Someone had once told him that if ever he felt like crying, he should do so as much as possible so he never cried for the same reason again. That was total rubbish. He had been crying in the shower every single morning for close to three months, yet the pain still felt fresh. He washed away his tears with the lukewarm water from the tiny bucket. When he walked out ten minutes later, he had his face to the ground, looking desperately for a place to hide his misery.

When Kuda walked into his room, his bed was already made. His father's Italian style black suit was laid out neatly on top, next to a sky-blue shirt and some cuff links, a black tie and clean charcoal grey stockings. He walked to the bed and got dressed, all the while, stealing glances at the small mirror that hung perilously on his wardrobe door. He pulled out his black formal shoes from under his bed and put them on before walking out.

"Oh, my son! You look just like your father. He would have been so proud of what a fine gentleman you have grown to be," his mother fixed his tie as she spoke.

She looked elegant in her United Methodist church uniform and matching handbag that hung gracefully on her shoulder. She picked Nkosi up and strapped him to her back. Mrs Dube led the way out and Kuda followed in silence. They waited by the road and in minutes, they had got a lift to Pearly Acres Memorial Garden.

"Have you gone over your speech?" Mrs Dube asked.

"Yes, ma," the lie came effortlessly. He had made his mind up some days back that he was not going to give a speech at the service. The only reason he had agreed to attend at all was to silence his mother who would not stop rambling about what impression it would give if he did not show up.

When they reached the memorial garden, everyone was already settled and listening to the preacher who swung his entire body around expressively as he spoke. He wore a black suit that was a size too small and his belly threatened to snap the buttons each time he moved. In his left hand was a water bottle and a handkerchief and he would occasionally pause to catch a breath. His deep voice roared out and echoed from all corners of the garden.

The guests were all dressed in black with their clothes contrasting perfectly with the white lilies that decorated the venue. They listened attentively to the preaching. Occasionally, an "Amen" would shoot out from one corner and heads nodded in agreement. Kuda's mother looked out of place in her blue uniform which drew even more attention to them than he had been hoping for. He was in an even tighter spot. All eyes followed his mother and him maliciously as the two trailed behind an usher to one of the front benches.

"Chin up my son," she whispered to Kuda who was, for the umpteenth time in those arduous three months, on the verge of tears.

They could feel all the eyes undressing them from behind as they sat in silence and listened along.

"I will now call upon the sisters of the deceased to uncover the tombstone," the preacher announced.

Kuda gazed distantly as Catherine and Mazvita walked to the front of the congregation. They reminded him of Tariro.

Mazvita especially looked like her sister, with her dark skin and bubbly personality. She had the same walk. The two girls moved gracefully in their silk dresses that kissed the tips of their shoes. They both wore matching coats and their faces were partially hidden beneath black nets. They slowly pulled away the white linen that had been covering the tombstone and Mazvita read out the epitaph inscribed on the granite:

In loving memory of Tariro Choto
A mother, daughter, sister and friend.
Born: 10 February 2000
Died: 16 June 2022
Forever in our hearts

As each word drifted out of Mazvita's mouth, Kuda felt an intensifying ache in his heart. The pain ignited a raging fire inside his chest and he could not breathe. He clenched his fists, the pressure he felt inside too much for him to handle.

"My Tariro is not dead. She will be back."

He broke out in tears as he charged towards the grave at full speed. Three pairs of hands grabbed him and pulled him back. It was as if they had been waiting for him to do just that.

"I knew inviting him was a bad idea," a voice echoed from the back. A few others grunted in agreement.

"She is not dead. My Tariro is not dead. What is wrong with you people?" Kuda cried out as the three men dragged him away. His mother followed silently with her face cast down as a breeze of murmurs undulated through the crowd. She walked briskly until she was out of the garden where Kuda had been tossed like a piece of garbage. She held him in her arms and rocked him as he cried his eyes out.

Mrs Dube spoke gently, "She is gone my son. Tariro is gone. I wish you were here when she passed. I wish you had seen her body lying in that box. Maybe then you would believe."

Her words only made him cry more bitterly. How was he simply supposed to believe that?

You had to do it

You were still five when you first noticed the tears in your mother's eyes, but a part of your young mind understood that things were not right. Your mother's voice trembled whenever your father appeared. You never questioned why, but you naturally snuggled into the fear and accepted the common, unspoken enemy.

At six, you watched as alcohol enticed your father into a crippling enslavement and you were left to bear testimony to how the treacherous liquid could sequester one's common sense from their mind to the point of no return. You vowed to yourself that never would a single drop of alcohol find its way to your lips. You wanted to be nothing like your father.

Tapiwa's father taught Tapiwa to ride a bicycle. Andrew's took Andrew to Mutarazi Falls in Nyanga for the greatest hike ever and Ngoni's dropped Ngoni off at school every morning in the coolest BMW. They all bragged about it during teatime and you smiled through their narrations, unable to relate to their flowery emotions. They too were eager to hear stories of how cool your dad was and each day you helplessly waited for him to give you a narrative worth sharing. The more you yearned for a piece of him, the more it hurt you because each day he seemed to drift farther from you.

By the time you were seven you had learnt to hate your father and the only thing you hated more than him was alcohol. A part of you yearned to believe that it was the alcohol that was solely responsible for his misdemeanours and that like you and your poor mother, he was also a victim in this story. But there had to be at least a speck of his conscience that was in touch with reality. A part of him had to be aware of the pain he was inflicting on you by having you endure his drunken actions and on your mother who bore the scars of his violent episodes and had to clean up after him. It was his smirk that made you hold the grudge against him; it reeked of a conscious satisfaction, and you hated him for it. Before you knew it, his presence had become a taste unpalatable to you. You knew that sooner or later you would have to spit him out. Yours was however an innocent type of hate. It was marinated in love and coated with compassion. You still hoped for change. You wanted your father to be better so you could explore the lengths to which you were capable of loving him.

On your eighth birthday, you watched as your father left home to go buy some milk for your mother's cooking. You would have wanted to go with him, but you had since stopped trying to ask. It had long been established that an unpremeditated no was what you would get. He made sure to shake off every last penny from your mother before he left. You wished he would smile at you, but he never even greeted you.

You waited by the window, hoping he would swing by any minute with your favourite toy, that fire truck you always admired each time you passed by your local kiosk or perhaps a cake. Yes, that would have been much better. You pictured it right to the last detail of its icing. "Happy Birthday Son," it would say on top and you would eagerly blow out the eight candles and wish for more stars in your mathematics book. By noon, your little spark of hope was dying out but you still kept your fingers crossed. Your mother tried to ease your aching heart. She made you the deep-fried *magwinya* dough balls you loved so much alongside her famous chicken chakalaka, but your appetite had vapoured away with your hopes, all fruits of your wishful thinking.

You would realise three weeks later, when your father finally showed up on a cold morning that it was indeed your hope that hurt you the most. You would watch in your sadness, his drunken body coiled at your doorstep, the memory of which is still vivid to this day. He has no milk, no fire truck nor birthday cake, only a half-filled bottle of Carling Black Label beer. His shoes are gone and so is the watch your mother got him for Christmas. He smells like a tavern. Flies flock to his pants and you know he has done it again; nature never lies. You fume with anger as you watch your mother wash him up. She does not allow a single word of complaint escape from her mouth and that makes your blood boil. You want her to yell at the top of her voice and throw a plate at the wall, but her calm is unyielding. A tsunami of anger and disappointment sweeps through you, but what can you do?

By the time you turn ten, everything has gone to waste except for your mother's patience. She still cleans after your father whose drunkenness worsens by the day. You watch helplessly as he hassles her for money to buy more beer. He sits around blessing his gut with alcohol while she tills the garden and vends her vegetables only to lose it all to him. You feel powerless, incapable of standing up to him and worse still, unable to care for your own mother. You share in her tears and your prayer each night is for your father to not make it to the next day. Each morning he wakes up with breath in his lungs is a disappointment to you.

Now you hate your father even more than ever but this time, the little love that had remained is gone. You are not sure if he even remembers your name. He only calls you boy when he needs another beer and demands you move with haste to display your respect for him. You have no recollection of the last time he looked you in the eye. He is just an antisocial stranger, trapped within the same walls as you and forced to occasionally acknowledge your presence. You avoid him as much as possible and as long as his beer needs are satisfied, he behaves likewise. You dare to muse that maybe deep down, he is aware of how much of a disgrace he is and that is why he shuts himself away from you. You no longer care about what he thinks or how he feels about anything. You just cannot stand him anymore.

You are twelve when you stand at the Warren Hills Cemetery, huddled in your mother's arms. Your eyes are dry but your soul is even drier. You disgracefully stare at all the mourners and you want to tell them to cut the act.

"*Mutungamirireiwo Yesu.*
Kuna Baba vedu kudenga.
Nzira yoko haaizivi.
Asinemi haakusviki!"

The Catholic Church choir breaks into marvellous song and you laugh at the irony of their gracefulness.

"Lead him oh Jesus.
To our Father in Heaven.
He knows not the way.
Without you he will not get there."

How dare they associate that monster with heaven? Clearly, they did not know him like you did so you do not blame them for their concern. They even say prayers for him and each positive word piques you.

In the distress of the funeral, the sense of relief overtakes you. The monster is really gone for good. You are however disappointed by your mother's tears. She mourns for a man that has pulled her back for years, the very same man who has made each second of her life a nightmare.

Pretty ungrateful.

After the sacrifices you have made to get here, the least she could do is force a smile. It not only took your time and effort but also guts to rescue her, but she is blinded. You feel her arms letting go of you and she rolls on the ground. For a moment you question if the decision to slide a couple of teaspoons of rat killer into his beer was a good one. You quickly get back to your senses. You have just done her the greatest favour ever.

He had to die.

The Christmas Surprise

The night's heat was unsettling. I floundered in bed and after several cycles of twisting and turning, threw away the blanket altogether. I sat up, reached towards the window, and cracked it open. I gave a subtle smile as a slight breeze hit my face.

"Can't sleep?" Pamela whispered from beside me.

I nodded in the darkness. She somehow got the message.

"Me too. I am so excited."

"Let's try to get some rest before morning breaks."

"Goodnight Sisi Chenge."

I turned to the other side and closed my eyes, but my mind would not shut down even for a second. I tried to stifle it but the excitement was getting the better of me. Christmas in Zviyambe had always been the highlight of our young lives but this year it would be far much better. Tete Tambudzai had sent word four weeks prior that she would be coming home.

Tete Tambudzai worked as a receptionist in Mutare. She had stayed and worked in the city for close to fifteen years. We had heard stories about the beautiful home she owned in Murambi. It was said she had even hired a man to take care of the lawn and garden. Tete was not married and we were the only family she ever had to be responsible for. She would send groceries every now and then. We would eagerly wait for the Tenda bus and receive our parcels. She always made sure to include gifts for everyone. The last time she had sent groceries, I had got a pink blouse which I wore with pride. Now that Tete was finally coming, it felt as if all the good things we ever dreamt of were finally coming.

The hours of the night slowly went by as I entertained my wildest thoughts. I had written to her saying I needed a dress and she had replied in her letter that she would get one for me. I pictured a floral dress with a brown belt. One that covered my legs down to the knees and danced gracefully in the wind. I could already see myself wearing the dress to church.

I was the first to get up on Christmas morning.

"Pamela! Pamela wake up!" I called out to my little sister who was still lingering in dreamland.

"I'm up! Christmas box, Sisi."

I smiled and gave her a hug. "Merry Christmas my dear."

With Pamela at my heels, I headed out of our bedroom. We picked up some reed brooms that were stored behind the kitchen and began to sweep the yard. I sprinkled some water over the ground first to moisten the soil so it would not be too dusty. Before we were done sweeping, Gogo walked out of her bedroom with a bright smile.

"Good morning *vazukuru*. Merry Christmas." As she greeted us, she drew each one of us in for a hug. Gogo was ever so jovial, but I could tell there was an extra scoop to her joyfulness.

She walked over to the boys' room and woke them up cheerfully. Since it was Christmas, no one would be going to the fields. Being an ardent Christian, Gogo believed in relaxing on Christmas day. She ordered the boys to go bath while she cleaned the kitchen and prepared breakfast.

I spotted a rooster race across the yard only to stand on one leg under one of the many mango trees that surrounded our homestead. Such a sight signified that a visitor was coming to the family. Today it meant more than it had ever done. It was confirmation that Tete was on her way.

As soon as Pamela and I were done sweeping the yard, we headed over to the bathroom. I made sure to take extra time lathering myself and taking in the freshness of the soap. Dressing up was always the best part of Christmas. I pulled out my pink blouse from Tete Tambudzai and straightened it out with a hot coal iron. I paired it with the black skirt Gogo had made for me. I applied curling gel to my hair and did the same for Pamela who looked like an angel in her white peplum dress.

We then sat in the kitchen for breakfast. Gogo had prepared scrambled eggs which we feasted on with bread and washed down with some creamy tea. She had also prepared some pumpkins, but because we had them nearly every day, we barely touched them in order to leave enough room for the bread. We cleared our plates and quickly cleaned up.

Soon after, Gogo gave each one of us a five dollar note. The family tradition was for all the children to go to the nearest shopping centre and treat themselves to some goodies. Gogo would save up all year in order to have enough money for us for the occasion. We were going to spend our quota while waiting for the bus that would bring Tete Tambudzai. I picked up the wheelbarrow that we would use to carry Tete's bags and groceries and led the way to the growth point.

We walked joyously to the Makarara Shops. They were about five kilometres away, but we had adapted to the distance which was almost the same amount we walked every day to school.

The shopping centre was a jungle of people when we arrived. Everyone was dressed in their best clothes and walked with a demeanour that spoke to excessive self-confidence. They were on the top of their game today. I saw a pair of boys walking out of a bottle store, Rodney and Ronaldo. I hated them. They always behaved like the self-appointed kings of Christmas. They wore black shades that completely obscured their eyes and matching white outfits and swaggered around like they owned the place. I watched silently as they walked to a Honda Fit that was parked close to where I stood with my siblings and our wheelbarrow.

Rodney broadened his smile and gestured for us to join them. I frowned and looked away. My esteem cried inside me. This was another part of every Christmas, one that I did not enjoy. I always felt like I looked good until I got to the shopping centre and compared myself with the other children. It was people like Rodney and Ronaldo that always made me feel inferior. We were clearly not in the same league.

Wait till our Tete Tambudzai gets here, I thought to myself.

I could not wait to pack all the groceries she would bring onto the wheelbarrow and wheel it home proudly while everyone watched.

We walked over to the Chiweshe grocery store. Mr Chiweshe was our favourite, and he knew each one of us by name. He always gave us free candy on Christmas. I placed the wheelbarrow on the veranda, and we walked in.

"Good morning, Mr Chiweshe. Merry Christmas," I greeted him respectfully.

"If it isn't my favourite squad," he chanted joyously as he patted each one of us on the shoulder, "come on in and feel at home."

We sat on the tiny bench by the wall in the store and looked around for what we wanted.

"I will get the lemon cream biscuits and a Fanta," I ordered as I handed him the crispy five dollar note I had.

"Enjoy!" Mr Chiweshe spoke as he handed me the things and a bottle opener.

"*Maita*," I cupped my hands in thanks as I received my treat.

The rest of the crew picked out their favourite snacks and we sat on the bench and dug into the food. We went for several rounds, from biscuits to chips to doughnuts. I bit happily into an oily doughnut and the sweetness of the cream on my tongue brought fullness to my heart.

"That's it folks. You are all out of money now," Mr Chiweshe finally informed us.

He handed each one of us candy sticks as we walked out.

"*Maita*," we all chanted in gratitude as we left.

The sun was nestled at the centre of the sky by the time we left the shop. Normally the bus would have arrived at this time, but it was late. We moved closer to the road and sat under the shade of a tree, our eagle eyes fixed down the road. Another hour passed and I could sense the impatience in the other people who also waited for the bus. The best thing that could happen for any family on Christmas day was to receive a visitor from the city. The worst was to wait for someone who would not show up.

The heat of the day intensified, and I could feel my sweat exploring hidden parts of my skin. I tried to fan myself with my hands to no avail. My anxiety worsened the feeling of being stifled. I gave an assuring smile to my little siblings who watched the road like their lives depended on it.

Another hour lapsed, and another and still the bus did not show up. I watched as some of the people who had been waiting lost hope and strolled away.

Murmurings about a possible accident began to grow and I grudgingly considered the possibility. Never had the bus been this late. I closed my eyes and made a silent prayer for Tete.

"Sisi Chenge, let's go home. It's getting dark," Pamela said as she held on to my hand.

"Just a minute," I replied while trying to conceal my anxiety.

The roaring of a heavy vehicle quickly grabbed our attention and all heads turned in the same direction.

"Look, there it is! The bus!" a voice erupted from the crowd and excitement quickly filled the air.

As soon as the bus stopped, people joyously scrambled around it and looked for their relatives.

I watched expectantly as each person got out. I stood on my toes to get a better view. When I spotted Tete, I let out a scream and went in for a tight hug. The crew behind me joined in.

"Welcome Tete," we choired out in joy.

"Let me hold this for you." I took the small shopping bag that was in her hands.

"Oh thank you, Chenge. You have grown into such a cultured young lady."

I gave her my best smile. Her words were music to my ears. I looked at all the people collecting their things from the luggage compartments of the bus.

"Where did you put your bags Tete?" I asked.

"That is all, honey. Shall we go home?"

Had she not been wearing a serious face when she said this, I would have thought it was a joke. I looked back at my wheelbarrow and felt a little shame. I placed the tiny shopping bag in the wheelbarrow and pushed it on.

The whole way Tete chatted with us. I did not say much. My mind tried to come up with explanations of where our cartons of groceries were. I wondered if Tete had forgotten to get us Christmas presents. I tried to picture whatever it was that was in the tiny bag she had brought. Maybe it was money. It had to be money. That is the only thing that made sense.

When we got home Gogo was anxiously waiting by the mango trees. As soon as she spotted us, she walked briskly towards us and hugged Tete Tambudzai.

"Oh my daughter, I missed you so much."

"I had missed you too, *mhamha*."

"Come on. I will make a cup of tea for you."

We walked behind Gogo and Tete as they slowly walked to the kitchen, arm in arm. It was getting a little dark and the kitchen was dimly lit. We sat on the floor and listened quietly to what Tete had to say. We were waiting for a big Christmas surprise.

Gogo picked a teapot and filled it with water. She gingerly walked to the fireplace.

"Ma, I got fired," Tete said.

Gogo dropped the teapot and gave Tete a piercing stare.

The witch must die

The moment she walked into our modest kitchen; I knew she was going to be a problem. Her smile was too perfect, her teeth whiter than anything I had ever seen and near flawless. I could tell it was too good to be true. I could see the frown beneath that smile. I played along though. I smiled back exaggeratedly, conscious of how much more yellow my teeth were compared to hers and that I was missing some of them. I loudly congratulated my brother, Benjamin for having found such a beautiful wife.

Observing from a distance, Chenai was perfect. Some people even went to the extent of calling her 'beautiful inside out'. I did not blame them for being fooled. Chenai not only had the perfect smile, but her curves were the envy of any woman who laid eyes on her. Her voice could take one to heaven and the moment she opened her mouth, one could not help falling for her. You could swear she bathed in milk seeing how rich her skin was. Her dimples were the cherry on top of the icing, and I was convinced that I was the only one she had failed to fool with her soft voice and superficial perfection. The only respite I had was that I did not have to bear her presence too often. Chenai stayed in Harare with Benjamin and occasionally they would visit us at the family homestead in Mhodzi Village. Those were not my favourite days but all it took was my practised smile to take me through the lengthy hours and days.

I knew when I received a call from Benjamin one day around three in the morning that things were not well.

"Sisi, Chenai and I are fighting," he said softly and I could hear the pain in his voice in the static of the phone call.

I smiled. I was tempted to pity my brother because I knew how much he loved her, but I had always felt that he deserved better. It was good that they were fighting. This could be the dawn of something great and the beginning of the end. Benjamin was too blinded to see anything. He had been cast under a spell. I held on to my phone and listened to him vent about how they both wanted a child so badly but had been facing challenges. Chenai insisted they visit a highly renowned *sangoma* she and her family had known for years, but Benjamin was adamant their situation was nothing a few visits to a fertility clinic could not fix. I capitalised on the opportunity and convinced him his opinion was the only one that made sense. Of course, I had to pour a little petroleum to the fire.

"I will pray for you, brother," I vowed just before hanging up but deep down I knew I would never pray for anything good to come out of their marriage. Not even if my life depended on it.

My intuition was not of this world and I had never been wrong about any person. I held on to my ideas of the world and people the same way I imagined I would cherish my degree had I gone through school. I could not read books but people. It came to me effortlessly. From the slightest interaction with a person, I could tell a lot about who they really were and where they had been. Chenai had been promptly blacklisted at first sight and I refused to feel bad for wanting my brother to be separated from a woman I could see would drag him down the drains.

I was even happier when rumours emerged that Chenai's mother had been accused of witchcraft. Some of them even went so far as to say Chenai had worked with her mother and I was only too happy that people were beginning to see her for what she was. I watched as my brother tried to protect her, but he too slowly grew tired of having to clear up the rumours.

"Sisi, tell me why I am only finding out today that Chenai once got pregnant but it had to be terminated due to complications?" When Benjamin made this call, I was certain he was finally done with her.

"That is why she refused to seek professional help," I emphasised from the other side of the line, hoping that my brother, in his rage, would make her pack her bags and leave.

"She knew, Sisi. She knew all along what the problem was yet she kept it hidden from me. She made a fool of me. I fasted and prayed for a miracle and she watched my misery in silence." Benjamin went on and on for an hour and I was happy his eyes were finally open. Chenai was a toxic liar and she deserved to be kicked out of his life.

But I was more disappointed when Benjamin called the next morning to say they had talked things out than I did on the day my boyfriend of three years stood me up saying he was going to come and pay my bride price. It was then that I was convinced my brother had been bewitched. It was the only thing that made sense. I had known Benjamin my whole life and he had been the spontaneous boy who did not take two seconds to deliberate his moves. Any slight inconvenience would trigger his full wrath and his decisions were always drastic and final.

For the next months I kept my fingers crossed, hoping my brother would snap out of his curse and redeem himself.

One day, Benjamin called to tell me he was moving to the USA for work.

"Chenai will be staying behind."

Those words were music to my ears.

Jackpot! Finally, the two would be separated. I was confident their relationship would not survive the long distance.

Then my mother came to me and gave a two-hour speech about how Chenai could easily get lonely in Harare and was better off living with us. I had celebrated too soon. MaSibanda insisted she wanted her daughter in law close by.

"This is a mistake."

"Life in the city without a husband or any kids will be so boring. Do you want your brother's wife to go out looking for boyfriends? Do you want her to be tempted by those dirty men of the city?"

My lips said no but deep down I would have preferred if Chenai remained in the city, imbibed in every delinquency of her choice.

Chenai knew I hated her and she made sure to return the same energy. The worst part was she had somehow managed to win MaSibanda's heart, so I quickly became the villain of the house. I changed my path each time I saw Chenai and she rolled her eyes each time I showed up. I pretended to not care but the wound of seeing my mother choose a woman she barely knew over me irked me. I endured the pain and held on.

It only took one strange night to change the order of our lives.

A wave of silence descended on our entire compound and the only thing disturbing the peace was the occasional frail hooting of an owl that had perched on the pinnacle of MaSibanda's hut.

I raced out of MaSibanda's sleeping hut around 2 am and headed to the kitchen from which I emerged less than a second later with a jar of water. I sprayed the cold water on her face while fighting to hold back the storm of tears that was already threatening to escape. My mother did not move. It was petrifying to see her in that state. Her jaw was wide open and locked and her fingers were clawed, veins imprinted all over her wrinkled skin.

"She is gone, Tete," Chenai spoke from behind me where she had been standing and watching.

"This is my mother! You might be willing to stand and watch her die but I will not do the same. I will not give up on her, she is all I have!" I shouted back before turning to the three little boys who stood in the freezing cold, watching me employ the rudimentary first aid skills I had picked up over the years.

"Call the neighbours! Call for help!"

All six feet raced towards the Ndengu homestead. I had never really had any regard for the little boys until then. They had been dumped by my older sister who was somewhere in the country, enjoying her life while we were forced to act in loco parentis to her fatherless children. I listened attentively with fingers crossed as the thumping footsteps quietened into the distance.

In minutes, the news had spread and the adults of the village cascaded to MaSibanda's hut. I was ordered out while an elderly woman assessed the situation. I walked to the back of the hut and cried. Even though no tragedy had yet been confirmed, I knew it already. For a couple of minutes, confusion stirred through the atmosphere as people waited for confirmation, for news of the inevitable that no one wanted to hear but everyone expected, until eventually, bitter screams tore from the tiny nucleus of villagers who had gathered. I knew then that it was final, that I would never get to taste MaSibanda's famous *nhopi* again or enjoy the warmth of her calm laughter. My heart shattered.

I had always pictured the day my mother would die. She always spoke about how things would be different after she was gone so it was inevitable. I imagined myself rolling on the ground in tears while the women of the village struggled to calm me down. The reality was far from anything that had ever crossed my mind. The pain I felt squeezed out every last bit of strength within me and my tears flowed silently.

I watched through cloudy eyes as women from surrounding compounds competed in their loud wailing. A woman in a lime head-wrap especially caught my attention and I immediately did not like her. Her wailing was the loudest, but never, during my thirty-two years with MaSibanda, had I seen her near our homestead. I had heard about dramatic mourners and now as I watched the pretence; it broke my heart even more. Of course, I felt worse because I was too calm for my liking, for someone who had just lost their mother. I struggled to make sense of everything that was happening.

The crying slowly subsided and it was overtaken by malicious murmurings.

"Someone sent an owl to kill her."

I had been told from an early age that the owl was an evil creature used by witches to spread turmoil, but I thought it was one of those things adults told children to scare them out of mischief, like if you sing while eating you become a thief. I never entertained the possibility that it was true and certainly never imagined such darkness visiting my own household. In no time, fingers were pointed and Chenai cast her face down to hide from the malevolent stares. I did not need to think twice about her possibly having a role in the death of MaSibanda. I only needed to prove it. It gave me consolation to know that the killer would one day suffer the consequences of her actions.

Chenai's highly envied glow had faded. She was not wearing her characteristic smile and there was no life in her eyes. A smirk settled on my face transiently when I saw her gloominess. Our village did not deal kindly with witches. Regardless of how law enforcement occasionally came through and tried to maintain order, witches were either stoned to death or burnt alive.

One thing was clear – MaSibanda's death was unnatural. I felt it in my bones that some evil was at play. Someone had killed my mother. I knew that person had to be Chenai and I could already imagine her agonised cries as large flames engulfed her. She was a witch and she had to die.

MaSibanda had been healthy. She had gone to the river that very afternoon in the company of our nephews to gather clay for her pottery and there had been no sign of frailty evident in her. That evening, she had prepared sorghum *sadza* and pumpkin leaves in peanut butter sauce. The entire family had feasted on the steamy mountains of food through smiles and giggles and made plans for the next day. MaSibanda was to go into the woods to gather *mopane* worms so that she would prepare yet another savoury meal for us.

"I will use a special recipe that I learnt from my own Grandmother," Masibanda had said and that was all the hype we needed.

The family had gone to bed on full bellies and grateful hearts. It had been the perfect night until Masibanda's moans of discomfort had summoned me.

Early in the morning, Masibanda's corpse was ferried to Mashinga District Hospital. One of the villagers offered his truck and accompanied by a few other villagers and I, we left the rest of the village in the company of their most toxic thoughts. Calls were made and the news about my mother's passing spread like wildfire. MaSibanda had been a people person so throngs of relatives and friends, came to our homestead for the wake. They were all devastated beyond words.

The sun had already spanned the length of the sky when I finally returned home. A post mortem had to be performed to find out the cause of her sudden death. We would be informed of the results the next day but, in the meantime, it only made sense to eye Chenai who never moved from her corner in the kitchen. Her eyes were swollen and red and her tears never seemed to rest.

Crocodile tears, everyone thought.

The tension in the air thickened when the call from the hospital finally came in. The elders of the family went to the hospital and came back with their faces cast down even more than they had been when they left. They had with them two police officers when they arrived to whom all eyes immediately rushed while all ears yearned to hear what they had found out.

A great silence befell the crowd when the cause of death was finally revealed. MaSibanda had been poisoned. The unfounded witchcraft accusations would now turn into a full-fledged murder investigation. I was the first to react. A horrified cry escaped from my mouth and the rest of the village echoed in turmoil.

"Sorry *wena*, sorry our child." Some of the older ladies of the village tried to comfort me.

What everyone saw was a loving daughter who mourned the death of her poor mother. Only I could perceive the depth of my anguish. Of course, I knew things no one else did.

***

A few days back, I had been in a heated argument with Chenai. She had complained about how I never put enough food on her plate and I had taken advantage of the situation to air out how I really felt about her.

"She is lazy but wants to eat a lot," I mocked. The argument had quickly escalated until I could hold my tongue no more and I spat out the words that felt like embers in my mouth, "You are a witch."

MaSibanda had finally interjected. As usual, she sided with her daughter in law and before I knew it, I was on the stand. I could feel my heart shatter. I loved my mother so much. I wished she would also see things the way I did. I wished she would pick my side.

In my anger, I walked into the woods in the scorching heat of the day. I walked aimlessly for hours. Gradually, sinister thoughts crept into my mind.

I walked up to a *rungozi* tree and began to dig. I knew the roots could kill whoever ingested them in a matter of hours. With tears in my eyes, I wrapped up the tiny chips of the dark plant in leaves and tied it into a knot with my wrapper. I would return home and act like everything was alright.

By the time I got home, MaSibanda was almost done preparing supper. I greeted her with a wide smile and even gave Chenai a hug which was reciprocated with a shrug. I sat by the side of the fire and spoke with my mother as she let her pot of sadza simmer. When she was done, she swept out some glazing pieces of charcoal and placed her pots on top so the food would remain hot after it had been removed from the fire.

As the family had always done on such nights, everyone went outside and sat on reed mats while they shared stories and laughed. I would normally lock myself up in my hut and not participate in these sessions. I hated how they would almost always end up being about Chenai shared stories about her childhood in the city of Bulawayo. For the first time in months, I took my own reed mat and joined the circle in silence. There was a lot of chatter and MaSibanda was especially delighted that I had voluntarily joined the family in good taste. I paid close attention to the stories told and watched as Chenai slowly invaded the conversation until eventually everyone was listening to her. They all loved her.

As the evening went on, it dawned on me that my family was not so bad after all. Life was not bad at all. All I needed was a little spotlight. I wanted Chenai's place. I wanted to be Chenai. My envy only fed into the diabolic thoughts that had been swirling around my head for hours now.

I listened quietly to the stories, my thoughts darkening like the sky before a storm.

"Vimbai, you can go dish out the food," MaSibanda instructed me. I leapt into the kitchen, closing the door behind me, and spread out the plates on the floor. I made sure to not hold back on the amount of food I put on Chenai's plate. Using a small knife, I scrapped some powder from the *rungozi* roots and mixed it with the vegetables in the plate. With careful urgency, I retied the rest of the roots into my wrapper in case I would need to use them again then I washed my hands and the small knife.

I called out to my little nephews to help me distribute the food.

"Take a jug of water over there and a bowl and make sure everyone washes their hands," I ordered the first.

"Give this to Chenai," I ordered the second while handing him a plate.

I remained in the kitchen until everyone had received their plate. I listened quietly as they prayed over the food. I silently prayed too... for mercy.

As soon as the "Amen" was said to conclude the prayer, a crippling weight gripped my chest and I could not breathe. I suddenly felt dizzy and my skin moistened in seconds. I walked out of the kitchen hoping no one would notice my anxiety. I walked to the back of the hut and sat down while trying to catch a breath.

"It will be fine. You will be fine," I kept whispering to myself.

My ears rang as I struggled to keep it together. I took multiple deep breaths. The faint laughter from the rest of the family echoed in my ears as I gradually settled down. The voices once again became vivid and I walked back into the kitchen like nothing had happened. I grabbed my plate then joined in the chatter and laughter as I dug into the steamy mountain of sadza.

When all plates were cleared and all the gossip exhausted, everyone retired to bed. I was tired but I failed to catch even a minute of sleep. I kept tossing on my reed mat until I decided to go outside for some air. It was then that the noise from MaSibanda's hut caught my attention and the ruckus began.

As the police spoke about what had killed MaSibanda and how they would get to the bottom of it, I felt my head spin and the contents of my gut churned. MaSibanda was dead while Chenai was still alive. It only meant one thing; a terrible mistake had been made with the plates. *I* was the witch I wished to see die.

Silk Haven

It was a smell she had grown so accustomed to, the smell of fresh blood. After countless nights of nursing the cuts and bruises her lover gifted her, the smell had become part of her daily routine. Now, it was accompanied by the sickening smell of burning rubber. Her ears rang and darkness shrouded her eyeballs. With every bit of energy she had left, Jane fought to overcome the resistance of her hugging eyelids and looked around. She was alive!

Before she could catch a breath, a frail cry emanated from where her legs were supposed to be. Jane realised she could not feel her legs, but she was more concerned about the cry.

"Mama," the voice cried out again.

Jane could tell from the sweetness wrapped around the small voice that it was a child, no older than five, the same age as the daughter she had left behind. The child's mother was likely among the lifeless masses of bloodied flesh that littered the tarmac. Tears welled up in her eyes. Her thoughts wandered to her daughter and she missed her now more than ever.

Jane had left home three years earlier when her daughter was a year old. She had many regrets in her life but being a teenage mother was not one of them. Even from a distance, she had thought of and prayed for her daughter each day and everything she had done was to give her child a better life. She loved her daughter, but she had done a dismal job in showing it. She, however, wished to change all that. It was fear that had driven her away in the first place; the fear of facing her mother each day and knowing that she was a disappointment; the fear of watching her own daughter grow up in poverty and not do anything about it.

The only feasible plan that had crossed Jane's mind was to travel to South Africa. She had seen people cross the border and come back a few months later with clothes, food and expensive appliances for their families and she decided to join the club. A couple of weeks of research landed her with a transporter who helped people like her to travel across countries without the required documentation. There was no way her mother would have agreed to such an arrangement, so Jane never bothered to tell her about it. Leaving only a note explaining where she was going and that she would be back in a few months with goodies, Jane left her widowed mother and her fatherless child in the hands of poverty with the hope of earning them a turnaround in life.

A small, white omnibus picked Jane up at Fourth Street Bus Terminus in Harare, together with a few other young ladies who looked a lot like her but more kempt and brighter. One of the girls went straight to sit in front and gave the driver a kiss and she had to be at least twenty years younger than the driver. Jane was tempted to frown but who was she to judge? She had mothered a child with a man who had to be at least in his early fifties, a man she had met only once at a drunken party. She looked away and watched the road. In a matter of minutes, they were out of Harare. Jane hugged her tiny bag and sat still in her seat.

"First time?" one of the young ladies asked with a subtle smile. "Oh, my name is Nakai. You are?" the lady continued before she had received an answer to her initial question.

Jane nodded and took two deep breaths before she spoke, "I'm Jane and yeah, this is actually my first time doing this. I am a little nervous I guess."

"The first time is always scary." Nakai giggled then continued, "You will be fine sis. I will look out for you."

"And you can always count on Dave," Nakai added, pointing at the driver.

Jane forced herself to find comfort in those words. Just by looking at Nakai; her ridiculously long nails, pink hair, unnaturally yellow skin and neon coloured outfit, she had concluded that she had to be one of those *slay queens* but maybe she had been too quick to judge. Maybe there was a lot of good beneath the physical drama. Jane smiled at the reassurance that things could possibly go well for her.

Nakai turned out to be a chatterbox and the conversation gradually transformed into a full-blown question and answer session. She was funny too and they found themselves in fits of laughter most of the way. The backroads they used were mostly bumpy, but the laughter diluted the discomfort. They made a few stops along the way only to go to the toilet and after what felt like a lifetime, they finally pulled over at a small growth point. Jane had no idea where she was. It was a couple of minutes after 7 pm and the girls cascaded into a small restaurant that stood next to a motel which was falling apart. Nakai, who claimed not to be hungry, remained behind with the driver.

Since she did not have much money to spare, Jane got a small Colcom pork pie and a Pepsi and quickly rushed back to the omnibus while the other ladies went through the menu and made their glamorous orders. She knew that something was terribly off when she got back and found Nakai wrapped up in Dave's arms in what appeared to be a very intimate moment. She immediately thought of the girl she had seen kissing Dave before they departed. Without saying a word, she walked away and found shelter in a nearby gazebo while the two busied themselves. She had hoped their detour would last only a few minutes, but it became increasingly apparent that no one was in a rush to set back on the journey. Her anxiety began to build up and she knew she had to make inquiries if at all they were going to make it to South Africa that day.

"Psst. Nakai," she whispered when she found the right opportunity to do so.

"Yes, baby *gail*?" Nakai had been speaking nasally and rolling her tongue exaggeratedly throughout their conversation but now her words were slurred.

"What's happening now? How long are we going to stick around here and act like we do not have somewhere to be?" Jane's patience had worn thin. She had been creating scenarios in her head of how she would work for a rich old lady in the suburbs and send piles of money, clothes and bologna to her mother and child. Her daughter especially loved the seasoned sausage ever since they had it for Christmas. The little one had sucked on it for hours and cried when the small piece was finally pulled out of her mouth and discarded. Sitting in a gazebo in the middle of nowhere added nothing to her prospects of achieving the goals she had set.

"You worry too much," Nakai replied, a bit more serious now. "We will spend the night here so don't worry. Dave is organising our rooms."

Had she had another option, Jane would have picked up her bags and left but her hands were tied. She was in an unfamiliar place with her life in the hands of people she had only just met and the only way forward was to sit back and watch where destiny would take her.

After a long hour and a half of waiting, Dave finally made arrangements for the night. A hostess ushered the girls to their rooms and as she had hoped, Jane got Nakai as her roommate. Eager to get some rest, Jane took a quick shower and quickly went to bed.

The night was calm and quiet. The wind, the bugs and the creeping creatures of the night seemed to be on a 'go-slow' demonstration. In spite of the peace of the night, Jane rolled over and struggled to get any proper sleep. She was anxious and her stomach churned. She would sit up for a couple of minutes to catch a breath then go back to rolling over in her blankets. It was well before 3 a.m. when the silence of the night was suddenly broken by rushed footsteps in the corridors. A couple of minutes later, a violent knock pounded on the door and Nakai rushed to get it.

"Time to hit the road, ladies. Get dressed. We have fifteen minutes," Dave spoke in an unsettled tone.

Nakai walked back and looked at Jane. Jane was a little perplexed and gave Nakai a look that desired an explanation.

"We have to cross the border before the break of dawn so we have to go now," Nakai said.

Jane pulled herself out of bed and in five minutes was ready to leave.

The other women were already in the car park when Jane walked out with Nakai. The omnibus they had used the previous day was nowhere in sight and in the poor lighting; they were packed into a greyish looking minibus. In minutes, they were on the road and Jane was filled with anxiety with a pinch of excitement. She was still sleepy but could not close her eyes even for a second because of the bumpiness of the road that found them being tossed up and about like popcorn on a hot plate.

The road seemed to go on and on and the silence in the vehicle magnified the enigma of the trip. The minibus eventually came to an abrupt stop in the middle of nowhere. The sky was only beginning to redden.

"Let's go ladies!" Dave shouted as he walked out of the vehicle. "Grab your bags. We are going to swim across the river. There is a team waiting for us on the other side. Follow the path that I take or else you won't make it across."

Those words filled Jane with fear but the other ladies seemed unaffected. She put up a firm face and played along.

I will do this for my daughter, Jane thought to herself as she strapped her bag to her back. Gingerly, she walked behind Dave and the other girls followed behind. She had expected the river to be shallow but as the water level inched up her body, she felt sweat trailing down her body into the ice-cold water. The rim of the river kissed the undersides of her breasts and she held her breath as she followed Dave further into the water. After twenty intense minutes of carefully manoeuvring the waters, they finally made it across and as Dave had said, there was another car with two men and a woman waiting on the other side.

"Welcome!" the lady exclaimed as she gave each one of them a hug. Her make-up was even louder than her voice and she reeked of an overused cheap perfume.

"My journey with you ends here. You are now in safe hands. Mrs Gobvu will take good care of you. She has a shelter for young women like you and I have already given her the necessary details so she can help you get jobs," Dave assured them before turning his back to leave. Jane was surprised to discover that she was a little saddened that he had to leave. He had, after all, delivered her to her salvation.

All six ladies were packed into the back of a Toyota Hilux twin cab and it drove away. The canopy blocked their view of the surroundings and it felt like they were on the road for an eternity. The car would stop after what felt like a lifetime and the girls were allowed to use the bushes for recess. At other stops they were not allowed to leave the car and were handed some take away food. The sun set and rose again and the long drive went on. After unending hours of bumps and turns, the car came to a halt and the ladies were finally ordered out. The sun was about to retire beyond the horizon when they arrived at what looked like a dormitory. It was surrounded by well aligned pine trees and there were no other houses in the proximity.

"Where are we?" Jane whispered to Nakai.

"Don't worry. We are safe here."

"You will be sharing rooms," Mrs Gobvu spoke as she handed a key to Nakai who winked at Jane. They would be roommates and Jane was happy she would stay with a familiar person.

As soon as they reached their room, Jane threw her tired body onto the bed and for a moment, remained frozen in the spot.

"You might want to take a shower. You will need it," Nakai giggled as she walked to the bathroom.

A shower would not be a bad idea. After Nakai was done with her long bath, Jane washed herself up. She felt the droplets of warm water massaging her skin and it eased her soul. For a few minutes she stopped thinking about her problems and absorbed the peace she felt around herself. Her next stop was Dreamland, wrapped up in soft linen. This was freedom at last and it felt good.

A loud knock on the door grabbed Jane from her sleep and she watched in confusion as Nakai walked to the door while fixing her nightgown. From her estimation, it must have been around midnight.

"Play along," Nakai whispered. "This is how we pay for our rooms."

The door gaped and two men, probably in their forties, walked in, bringing with them a strong smell of alcohol.

"Hey baby girl. We had missed you. How was Zimbabwe?" one of them spoke as he rubbed Nakai's neck.

A paralysing chill ran through Jane's nerves. She knew without explanation what she had got herself into. Nakai seemed to know what she was doing. She engaged the men in a rather too giggly conversation and occasionally gave Jane angry glances for sitting in silence.

"Is she new here?" one of the men asked while looking at Jane.

"Yes," Nakai replied. "Jane just got in from Zimbabwe. She will loosen up, don't worry."

"She better," he said, "We are not paying for nothing."

Nakai tried to lighten the atmosphere. She would try as much as possible to incorporate Jane in the conversations. She eventually began to focus her attention on one of the men before finally walking out with him, leaving Jane with the other. A wave of silence followed their departure.

Fear took over as Jane watched her new roommate lustfully lick his lips and move closer to her.

"Give me a massage," he commanded in the hoarse voice of someone who knew they were in charge.

Jane pulled herself together and rubbed his firm shoulders. He kept talking about his mining claims and how much money he was making from his investments. Jane would nod and agree to whatever he had to say until, to her relief, he passed out on the couch. She spent the rest of the night sitting on her bed thinking about what would become of her.

Jane had not signed up to be a sex worker. She did not exactly have an honourable track record in her sexual life, but she had promised herself to do better. She had made a vow of celibacy and had held on to it since the birth of her child. She was not about to disregard the most important promise she had made to herself.

Run for your life! The thought kept Jane company as she reflected on what she would do next.

She knew she had to leave as soon as possible. As she thought more about it, she realised, with mounting horror, that there was a chance she was not in South Africa at all. The men had a peculiar accent, if only she could pin it somewhere on the map. No one in this place was to be trusted, not even Nakai. *Did she know? Was she also a victim? No.* Nakai had seemed a little too confident to be an amateur. Jane blamed herself for having been fooled and she wished she had just stayed at home and endured her mother's disgust. She decided she was going to run. There had to be someone who could help. Maybe a household somewhere down the road.

When morning broke, Jane was so relieved that she had not been forced to have sex with anyone. She was careful not to so much as hint that she was deliberating leaving the place and the whole operation. Breakfast was served and all the girls were assembled in one huge dining hall. There were girls of different ages and form and they each seemed to be happy and at peace. Jane scanned for a friendly face and spotted a fair skinned girl with curled ginger hair. She walked up to her and introduced herself before getting into what she was after.

"Where are we?" Jane whispered.

"You are not allowed to ask such questions here. If you want to make it in this place, you need to keep your mouth shut," the ginger haired girl replied before walking away.

Jane knew now for certain that she had been fooled. She forged a smile and pretended to go along with what was happening.

Mrs Gobvu walked into the room and the atmosphere toned down into deep silence.

"Good morning my girls," she spoke with pride. "We have a few new members with us today. May they raise their hands?"

Jane reluctantly pushed her hand up.

"Let's give them a warm welcome to the sisterhood!"

The room broke into applause before abruptly falling back into the silence.

"Now I understand that each one of you is here for a unique reason," Mrs Gobvu went on.

"Some of you ran away from poverty, some of you were abused at home and some of you just needed a breath of fresh air. Here at Silk Haven, we give young women like you a second chance at life. You will be able to make the money that you wish to have. If you work really hard, you can make up to thousands each month. For the first three months here, you will not get a salary to cover for your travel and accommodation costs but from then onwards, you will begin to get paid and we will even facilitate for you to send money back home. Like any other place, we have a couple of rules here:

    1. You always use protection.

    2. Only I handle the money.

3. You can only leave after working for three months to cover for the money we invest in you by facilitating your travel."

When the address was over, the girls lined up to get food. While everyone busied themselves with filling their bellies, Jane analysed the place. The main gate was just in front of the dining hall and there was a guard stationed there. She had however noticed on her way to the dining hall that there was a small orchard behind the building. If she could climb over that fence unnoticed, she might be able to run away.

Jane walked to one of the ladies who seemed to work at the place and complained about a stomach ache so she could be excused. Back in her room, she had not yet unpacked her belongings, so she simply grabbed her bag and hid it behind a trash can outside the dormitory. She watched all movements throughout the day and when the sun finally crawled into hiding, she grabbed her bag and ran towards the orchard. In five minutes, she was out of the yard and running through the woods. She kept just close enough to the road to not get lost but did not use it.

After close to two hours of running and walking without meeting a single soul, she eventually came to what looked like a tuckshop. A few people were sitting around a fire, listening to music. When she got closer, she found that they spoke in a foreign language that she could not place. While she was still trying to decide which of them to approach, the store keeper called out to her from inside.

"Everything ok young lady?"

She walked to the shop, feeling the eyes of the group on her.

"Sorry sir, I am lost. If you could tell me where I am and how I can get to the nearest town"

The old man laughed. "You are in Siwela Village. There is only one bus that goes to town and it passes through here at five in the morning. I am afraid you will have to wait till tomorrow."

Jane's face fell. She needed to be out of here as quickly as possible.

"Isn't there another way sir?"

"I'm afraid not, my daughter. I can speak to my wife and we can accommodate you for the night. In the meantime, you can sit by the fire with the others. Here's a coke. Just relax."

Jane cupped her hands and clapped in gratitude before receiving the coke and walking to the circle. She sat in silence while the group continued to chat and roast mealies. She had been sitting for about half an hour when a grey Toyota Hilux pulled up at the tuckshop. She immediately recognised the car in the glare of the fire. Mrs Gobvu walked out with the grimmest of expressions on her face. She had two other men with her who grabbed Jane and pulled her into the car.

"Save me! Help!" Jane screamed her lungs out.

She could tell from the sealed lips all around that no one would come to her rescue.

"Thank you," Mrs Gobvu spoke to the owner of the tuckshop before turning to Jane.

"You ungrateful fool. You think you are clever huh. You think you are so special," Mrs Gobvu screamed in the car while tears rolled out of Jane's eyes.

When she got to the compound, news about her attempted escape had already spread. She could tell from the malevolent stares she got that the other girls despised her. Others giggled and mocked her. Her heart sank. She was not going anywhere anytime soon.

The system at the dormitory was rigged against the women whose bodies were used for profit making, yet they all stayed for various reasons. Most had been brought in under the impression of going to greener pastures, as Jane had, only to realise they had to work for three months to cover the costs of their travel to get there. After the unpaid months, more reasons to stay came and the bureaucracy kept the ladies trapped. They would eventually adapt to the systems and gradually, a little more money went into their pockets. Things would probably be harder elsewhere. It was a relatively lucrative business although the investors behind the scenes had more to benefit from it than the ladies on the ground.

Jane hated the job. She had never imagined that she would one day have to use her genitals as a source of survival and now here she was. Man after man, she hated herself even more and despised everything about her life. She could not wait for her three months to end so she could get away. Each night, cavalcades of expensive cars drove into the compound and the girls were lined up and handpicked by the men. Jane kept no recollection of her clients and only viewed her work as a transaction, a step closer to freedom. Until two months later.

"Kevin. My name is Kevin," he spoke with a swagger that knocked the common sense out of her. She immediately knew that he would be more than just her customer. He was charming and instead of tossing her body around like all the other men did, he spent the night in conversation with her. It was as if he was trying to read her soul. No man had ever made her feel this way – seen. It felt good. She helplessly fell in love with him.

In a night, Jane had learnt everything she needed to know about him. Kevin was a businessman in the logistics industry. He had his own trucking company which was doing quite well. He was not married yet but felt it was time to enter a serious relationship. According to him, a voice in his head had led him straight to her and he insisted meeting her was no coincidence. This was not the conventional place to find true love, yet he was convinced that she was the one. By the break of dawn, he had convinced her to leave behind her cheap life and start a new one with him. She couldn't say no. She was broke, desperate and a rich man had been delivered to her on a silver platter.

"Meet me at the *mopane* tree down the road," Kevin said before he left.

Jane had to be strategic. While everyone was having breakfast, she set on the route she had used the first time she had tried to escape and found Kevin waiting for her as he had promised. They drove for hours before they reached the city.

"Welcome to Maputo, babe," Kevin spoke as he looked at her through gentle eyes.

Kevin booked a lodge at the heart of the city and stayed there with Jane for a few days. Afterwards, he rented an apartment for her which was fully furnished with everything she needed. All she had to do was be his unofficial wife and he would keep providing everything for her. He even made arrangements to have her send money home via the post office. Jane managed to get in touch with a neighbour who confirmed her mother received the money. Her mother had no phone and refused to have any direct communication with her. She would only pass the message that she was grateful for the money but beyond that, she said nothing else.

Jane knew her mother was displeased with her, but she had to do what she had to do to give them a life.

The life she had with Kevin was better than anything she could have imagined. It was almost perfect. One thing, however, worried her. Kevin never wanted Jane to leave the house for any reason except when she was in his company. The idea of leaving the country to visit her mother and daughter was a non-starter. She needed his money and so she had to bow down to his rule. She forced herself to be an introvert and stayed behind closed doors for hours without complaining.

Months went by and true to their arrangement, Jane continued to get her handouts and pass them on to her family. She missed them, but she never wanted them to know how she was sustaining her new life. Each day, her longing to be with her family intensified. She felt herself gradually tire of being the forced stay-at-home wife that lived on handouts.

After days of deliberating, Jane finally decided to flee and return to her family. If it meant they would fall back into deep poverty, they would fight it as a family as long as she was in a place where she knew she really belonged.

It was around midday when Jane picked up her bag. She looked around the house and thought of all the memories she had created there. They were recollections of a subtle imprisonment. It had all been worth it though. She had taken care of her family but now she would finally reunite with them. Kevin would be at work till around 5 pm. She walked out of the house nonchalantly.

When she was only a few metres away from the gate, a black Navara approached Jane and she froze in horror. Her heart skipped a beat and she took a deep breath before turning back to the gate with her bags.

"Hey love. Wait up. Were you gonna go on a trip without me?" Kevin mocked as he approached her. The sarcasm in his voice was clear.

She could not say a word. She could only face the ground in disgrace.

"Let me help you with those," Kevin said as he took the bags and walked back to their apartment. Jane followed in silence. She took the keys from the flowerpot in which she had left them and unlocked the room. She hesitantly walked in with Kevin behind her. She knew she had a lot of explaining to do.

"Kevin I..." He abruptly dropped the bags, pulled her braids and swung her to the wall. She landed on it, forehead first, with a thud and he threw a punch right at her face. "Kevin! Kevin!" she screamed as he once again tugged her braids and swung her, this time to the floor. The metallic taste of blood invaded her mouth as she lay on the floor and he kicked the thoughts of freedom out of her.

"You ungrateful slut," he kept saying as he hit her. "I feed you. I give you a place to stay. I even take care of your stupid mother and your bastard. Is this how you repay me, huh?"

Jane had never seen this side of Kevin and it broke her heart. Her emotional pain exceeded her physical aches.

Each day that followed came with a serving of some beating to remind her of how bad things could get if she ever tried to escape again. But for all his efforts and threats, Kevin only succeeded in making her more determined to leave. Her womb cried out to her daughter and she was not about to give up. Kevin kept her under lock and key. If ever she was going to make it out alive, she would have to do so while Kevin was around. Eventually, she came up with a plan.

On a very fine Wednesday evening, Jane waited for Kevin to get home. She wore a purple, body hugging Fashionova dress that matched her lipstick and eyeshadow. She prepared a roast turkey and gathered all the alcohol she could find in the house; the beers in the fridge and the whiskeys that Kevin occasionally brought with him.

Kevin fell right under her spell. He did not scream at her about how ungrateful she was as had become the norm. She kept his glass of alcohol full, waiting for the right moment. When she sensed the alcohol had got to his head, she rocked him to sleep. As soon as he dozed off, Jane gingerly slipped her hand into his pocket and pulled out the key. She walked to the bedroom and pulled out the tiny bag she had already packed and hidden in the closet. She tip-toed to the door and gently turned the key. A hushed sigh of relief escaped from her mouth as the lock clicked open. As she softly pulled the door handle, a rough hand gripped her neck.

"I guess you never learn," Kevin barked from behind her and threw her against the wall. She felt her head crash into the bricks and her brain made a little sad dance within its cavity.

"Kevin no!" she cried as he walked towards her. He clasped his hands around her neck and squeezed.

She could barely breathe and she could feel a stream of blood run down from her left nostril. It felt like she was in the closing scene of a movie, just before everything faded to black, one in which she would die without saying goodbye to her family, leaving them with nothing but scars of disappointment.

Jane clamoured for air and swung her hands all over the place, looking for something, anything, to hold on to. Eventually, she felt the cool, smooth surface of a bottle and she did not think twice as her fingers coiled around it. She gathered all her strength and swung it in the direction of Kevin's head. It landed with a sickening thud and his skull gave in. With a loud cry, he let go of her and clutched his occiput. Jane took another bottle and went for his head again and again until all she could hear was a faint, laboured groaning and the shattering of glass as she took one bottle after another and pounded. She was in a trance. When she finally snapped out of it, she knew she was in trouble.

There was blood everywhere. The white floor tiles were a pool of blood, his head was blood and her dress was blood. It partly felt good to not be the one whose blood would stain the floor for a change, but she had just killed a man. She was a murderer now.

Jane was faced with two options; she could run and find her way out of the country before the police got to her. After all, the house was in Kevin's name and she never got visitors so no one could place her here. Or she could sit around and wait for the consequences of her actions to catch up with her. It was not an option at all.

What good would it do her to be imprisoned and rot behind bars in a foreign land? She had to go home. For her daughter she had to try.

Jane cleaned herself up and locking the door behind her, left Kevin's corpse in its pool of blood. She caught a bus and found herself on her way to Zimbabwe. She still did not have the required documentation but with guts and a couple of bribes, she knew she would find her way across the border.

As she had hoped, the bus driver was familiar with people who illegally crossed the border and he agreed to help her. He would do most of the talking, smooth out the process for her. At times the negotiations took minutes or even hours but eventually everything worked out. After what felt like an eternity, Jane was overjoyed to find herself looking upon the familiar sights of Zimbabwe.

She looked out through the window and felt relieved. At last, freedom. She would no longer have to sleep with men to get food on her table. She would be reunited with her family again.

She thought of her daughter and her heart sank. She wondered what kind of a girl she had turned out to be and she hoped she would get to make up for the time they had lost. She vowed never to leave her family again. Never!

The bus made a stop in Mutare and the passengers busied themselves getting refreshments. Jane remained in her seat and marvelled at the bustle until one vendor caught her eye. He had dolls of different shapes and sizes lined in his wheelbarrow and a backpack with other fluffy toys. Jane decided to get something for her daughter.

"Psst Baba! How much for the bear?" Jane pointed at a beige teddy bear.

"Five dollars my daughter."

Jane opened her wallet and pulled out five clean one-dollar notes. She handed the money to the vendor and received the teddy bear.

Shortly after, the bus was on the road again. Jane held on to the teddy bear and kept thinking of her daughter. Gradually, she felt herself dozing away and the conversations around her became fainter. She was half asleep when the screams of the other passengers woke her. She watched in horror as the bus veered off the road, missing a vegetable truck by an inch. The bus headed for a tree before making a dramatic turn then crashing into a boulder and rolling back towards the road.

"My leg! My leg!"

"My baby"

"Oh Lord"

Many such screams filled the air alongside the incomprehensible cries that came out as mourns and groans as the bus rolled over a second time and a third. Jane felt her head banging into metal bars countless times. Everything went dark.

When Jane regained consciousness, the smell of fresh blood was doused over everything. With her legs paralysed and her entire body in pain, Jane felt she was being punished for her sins.

***

After three days in the hospital, Jane was on the verge of a breakdown. Other people who had been involved in the accident with her had had their relatives coming to see them, but no one had come for her. She had sent word to her mother of her tragedy but she still had not shown up. She was finally told she had a visitor.

She watched with tears in her eyes as her mother walked in with a little girl running behind her. Jane wished she could leap up and rush to hug them but the weakness in her legs would not allow it. Instead, she let out a single, loud cry that expressed all of her joy, relief, pain, regret, trauma, fear and helplessness. Her mother wrapped her arms around her as she too cried.

"I am here now my baby. Everything will be alright. Aisha is here too." She opened up her arms so all three could hug each other.

Jane wanted to apologise for having left. She wanted to tell her mother and her daughter how much she loved them and how she had missed them every single day. She wanted to tell them what she had been through from the time she had left. She wished to tell her mother what she had had to do to be reunited with them and how the consequences could catch up with her. But all she could do was cry. Her heart was at ease. She was home.

A day in my shoes

It's six in the morning. The cock crows. While the rest of mankind come alive, I wipe away tears as I battle with the small fire in our dingy zinc roofed kitchen. Power cuts have become an indefinite part of life, leaving firewood as our only option. Raised by a single mother who is battling with AIDS, I have to be up early enough to clean up and cook before going to school. Bathing daily is a luxury considering the scarcity of water and the absence of soap.

Mama pulls out a two dollar note from under her pillow. "My baby, today you can board a *kombi* to school," she says with a warm glow on her wrinkled face. This is the combination of words I wish to hear each morning but seldom ever do.

I make my way to the bus station with a beaming smile on my face. Today is my day, I can feel it. I can barely contain the excitement. After a long wait, the *kombi* finally arrives. The conductor sticks out half of his body through the window and yells, "Four dollars to Tandi School!" Of course, the price has doubled overnight but unfortunately, it's June, so no Christmas miracle is coming my way. "Not today kid," the conductor says looking at my tattered green note in disgust as the kombi drives away.

Inclining my eyes towards the skies so gravity can hold back the tears, I jog towards school which is fourteen kilometres away. I have never owned a watch in my life, but I do have my own way of telling when I am terribly late. I picture myself being canned for the fifth time in a row for showing up late to school. As my tiny bare feet hit against the ice-cold, potholed tarmac, I can feel the pain radiating from the smallest of my toes to my skull. I pass by three other schools in my ghetto which my mother cannot afford. To be honest, she cannot afford anything. I don't even remember the last time my fees was paid and now I am stuck at the only school in the district which tolerates such behaviour.

As I manoeuvre the streets, it is difficult to tell if I am still in an urban area or not. At one corner, someone is selling goats and road runners, at another, someone has sugarcane and at the other, there are piles of firewood. People are desperate to make a living and at this point, no hustle is too small. Already I have passed by ten vendors, each chanting a unique marketing song as they move around with their goods. For a second, I think of the good old days when mom was fit enough to join the bustle of hustlers. The memories thaw my heart a little and I almost smile, but the pain of reality spares me no second. I frown at the thought of how we now depend on the little I get from serving at the nearby farms during weekends. Life is indeed a hike on thorns for me.

I get past the residential areas and delve through thick woods, pushing to make myself believe I am totally safe as I struggle to suppress the fear that is seated deep within me. Finally, I get to school and I am just on time. Just on time for the tea break. I wonder why they call it a tea break when we never get any tea. The privileged devour their packed meals while I pretend to resent food. I have missed the morning lessons and it turns out no one sympathises with me. I am awaited by good news and bad news. The good news is my teacher is sick and tired of beating me and so today I have escaped her wrath. The bad news is a decision has been made to surrender me to the headmaster, a four eyed nightmare, for disciplining. I feel a strong urge to say, "Try putting yourself in my shoes" but unfortunately, I don't own any and that murders my confidence. Instead, I clutch the hem of my ragged dress in a clenched fist as I push back the tears.

Sixty per cent of my time in class passes by as I doze. I am tired. How could I not be? I am that unpaid housemaid who has walked fourteen kilometres on a porridge breakfast. Hopeless. That is what they have nicknamed me in class. My teacher goes through my homework book with the same look of disgust with which she always responds to my presence and all she can say is, "They do not pay me enough to deal with this rubbish!" Rubbish? Really? Easy for her to say. I barely slept trying to get it done using a candle. If only for a second, the world would experience life from my end.

As soon as the final bell rings, I quickly get on my way home. This is the one thing in my life that I lead, the way out of school. I am well aware of the sorry situation that lies ahead. I have to get home and fetch enough water for the night and the next day from a borehole that is far away from where I stay. I have to stand in line for hours for a supply of water from the municipal borehole. I have to cook and clean Mama up. These days she barely leaves her blankets. On especially bad days, the blankets are also her toilet. I am all Mama has left and I will do anything to take care of her. Basically, the sight at home when I leave in the morning is the same thing that awaits when I return, if not worse. I still do all the work with no complaints. I am aware of how deep we are in debt and so I keep my fingers crossed hoping that the landlord will not drop by any moment. After all the struggle, I still have to do my homework before I call it a day.

Minutes after midnight, I finally close my eyes to rest. Silently, I pray for a better tomorrow. Through it all, I still believe that one day life will get better. This is a day in my invisible shoes.

And in sickness

The doctor spoke about the lesion in my brain that he had seen on the CT scan, but it did not bother me. He went on and on about how complicated and expensive the required surgical intervention would be but that did not move me either. I was equally unmoved by the fact that I had pending medical bills that required payment. I remained silent as the crew in white coats asked questions about my financial background, and I could tell they resented me for my lack of enthusiasm. My mind was far from the ward. I was lost in my ugly thoughts.

Shantel had missed the morning visit, and that was unlike her. She had not come for the evening visit the previous day and I had been anxious ever since. Over the past two weeks, she had been acting a little off but missing a hospital visit was a stretch. I kept checking my phone and she had not called or texted. My Shantel had always been time conscious and would not miss an opportunity to spend time with me for anything. I failed to make sense of whatever was going on. In my five weeks of admission at Harare Hospital, she had never gone silent without an explanation and so I started to fear for her life. When Doctor Mboweni was done evaluating my case, he moved away with the group of medical students that trailed behind him on to the next patient. I began my countdown to the lunchtime visit.

As soon as the doors opened to visitors, my mother walked in in her agitated, fast-paced step.

"Has she contacted you yet?" my mother asked before she sat on the small bench by the bedside.

I only shook my head, then thanked her for the bananas she had brought with her.

"She is up to no good. That wife of yours is up to no good. I can feel it in my veins."

"Stop, *mhamha*. I am already stressed, and you are only making it worse."

"She has another man. Don't say I didn't warn you."

Immediately, I felt a numbing feeling in my gut and I looked towards the window. I refused to accept it but the same thought had also crossed my mind. Shantel had been calling and texting me less than usual over the past several days. Before I could fully put my thoughts in order, Shantel briskly walked in. She was sweaty, could barely breathe, and her blouse was half untucked. It was clear she had been in a hurry.

"I am so sorry sweetheart," she emphasised as she came right over to the bed and rubbed my head.

The air of relief I felt was quickly tarnished by the strong smell of Lagerfeld cologne that came from her. I knew it very well because my former manager had used the same cologne and it brought back an unpleasant nostalgia. I had always been aggrieved by the way he treated me. What worried me more was the fact that I knew I could never afford the cologne, and neither could Shantel. Had my wife really come to visit, reeking of another man?

I watched as Shantel unpacked the food she had brought. She had a Steers paper bag and I could not help but wonder where she had got the money to waste on fast food. I did not have it in me to confront her. The best I could do was to reject the food and blame it on nausea.

When the visit hour lapsed, I was left with more questions than before she came. I stared blankly at the ceiling, hoping my thoughts would come to rest and allow me to sleep. Amid my torment, a nurse walked up to me. She wore a slightly yellowish smile from ear to ear and it brought out a dimple on her left cheek.

"How are you feeling now, sir?"

I raised my thumb but did not let out any sound.

"I have great news, sir. Your hospital bill has been settled and a well-wisher has offered to sponsor your surgery. Dr Mboweni has instructed me to set a date and you can have the surgery done on Friday next week."

"Do you know who this well-wisher is?" I asked.

"No sir. He has chosen to remain anonymous. I guess it's your lucky day."

I felt an overwhelming wave of joy bubbling within me. I had to say a prayer of thanksgiving first then call Shantel.

I found my phone under the blanket and began to dial. Before I could make the call, another thought came to mind and my little flame immediately died down. I decided to call my friend Tawanda instead.

"Hi Tawanda, how are you?" I spoke with a firmness I hoped would hide the confusion that was drowning me.

"Hey bro!" Tawanda spoke with his usual jovial tone. "How are you doing? How are you feeling today?"

"I feel a bit better than usual. Look, man. I need a favour."

"Anything for you, bro. What's up?"

"Something dodgy is going on. I need you to follow Shantel around just for a day. Someone is giving her money. I need to know who it is and why they're doing it."

"*Hai* man. That is too big a favour to ask, even for you. I respect Shantel. Please man, no," Tawanda protested.

"Do this for me and I will never ask anything of you again."

I knew I was putting my friend in a tight spot, but the lack of clarity kept me in distress. Tawanda was not one to indulge in any vices and he had always tried to stay on the path of morality. If I had another option, I would have gone for it but he was my only hope at finding the truth and so I pestered him until he agreed to help.

Even though I had asked for Tawanda's help, a part of me already sensed the truth. I could not get over the possibility that I was being catered for by my wife's lover's money.

The next morning, I messaged Shantel and asked about her plans for the day. She was going to first visit me, then go home to do laundry. She would then come back to the hospital during lunchtime, then go home to rest before the last visit of the day.

I waited anxiously for Tawanda to prove my suspicions right. That day, she did not miss any of the visits. She was on time and did everything as she had told me she would throughout the day. It was almost as if the universe had tipped her off on what was happening.

That evening when Tawanda called, my heart broke, not because he had found anything of concern, but because I wanted to be right so bad. The disappointment of having failed to catch her in a corner ate me up. I was still convinced she was being unfaithful.

"Shantel is a good woman. You can't be doing this to her," Tawanda defended her.

"One more day please," I found myself begging again until Tawanda agreed to take up the task. To my disappointment, when the second day ended, he still had no evidence of foul play.

"You need to work on your marriage. All these suspicions will not do you any good," Tawanda advised, but I would not listen to him.

"I just need you to try one last time," I pleaded with him.

"No. I am done being your spy."

"Please man. Just this once," I said without hiding my desperation. "You know I would do the same for you if you were in my position."

Tawanda went silent for a while, then with a deep sigh, finally agreed to help.

"I hope you won't regret this," he said before hanging up.

That Thursday morning, I messaged Shantel again about her plans for the day. She did not reply. She had mentioned something about a choir practice during our last conversation, but that would not be until midday. That day, she did not show up for the morning and afternoon hospital visits. I dared not call or ask about it.

A few hours before the evening visit hour, I received a text from Tawanda.

"I am sorry bro, your suspicions were right. Shantel is seeing someone. She spent the whole day with a man in Marlborough. I did a little research and it turns out she has been spotted with this man a couple of times. She has even spent nights at his house."

A picture was attached to the text and I zoomed into it. The picture was dominantly occupied by a rosewood Range Rover and in the extreme left corner stood a man who looked like a shorter version of my father. His balding head glared in the sun with a dark pair of shades balanced above his eyebrows. Besides the car, he was no better than I was. He was a ted too dark for the lime sweatshirt he wore. The whole time I avoided Shantel, whose hands rested on his shoulders.

Her blonde braids were scattered all over his sweatshirt. I did not want to look at her face. I was afraid she would be looking happier than I could have ever afforded to make her. I threw my phone aside and allowed myself to fully experience the shiver that took over my entire body. Even though I had seen it coming, I found it hard to digest the fact that Shantel would actually cheat on me.

When Shantel walked in for the evening visit, I could not look at her the same. I wanted to snap at her the moment she got to my cubicle, but she beat me to it.

"So, you sent someone to spy on me? After everything I have been doing for you?" she screamed her lungs out.

"Oh, shut up you cheating whore," I charged back.

"You are so ungrateful. I can't believe you!"

The other visitors stared and the nurses started coming in to settle the chaos.

"Ma'am, you might want to keep it down or we will be forced to kick you out."

Shantel quieted down and I spoke my case.

"I want you to look me in the eye and tell me you didn't sleep with that man."

She looked at me and remained silent. "I thought as much," I spoke on while trying hard to hold back my tears.

"Babe this is unfair. I did this for you. I did it for us." She paused to breathe. "You need this surgery. I am not ready to lose you." She was on the verge of tears.

"I don't want anything to do with you or your dirty money."

"Babe, please. Don't be like this."

"Shantel. Please leave. We're done."

She looked at me through her red teary eyes. I looked away and entertained my own tears. I heard her footsteps moving away and my soul cried out in despair.

Beneath this thick skin

From the word go, Namatai had not been a conventional village girl. Her cooking was terrible. She never bothered to learn how to do her hair like her sisters had and scruffiness came naturally to her. She was taller than her sisters and she always stooped her shoulders as if to hide her height. She had been gifted with an extra dose of melanin and her voice was rather hoarse. She had calves that protruded beyond her buttocks and her biceps stood out. Her veins could easily be traced along her arms. By all accounts, she had the body of a man. Many a times, Namatai would be seen playing with the boys. She preferred herding livestock to cleaning with the other girls. Occasionally, she would be involved in fights at the pasture fields. And she was not one to lose. As she grew, her mother always made jokes about how the heavens had not given her a son but had brought one out in her youngest daughter.

Namatai not only competed with the boys in her physical strength, but she was also gifted academically. Unlike the other girls of the village who dropped out of school before or in the early years of high school, she was determined to progress academically. Her parents thought it was only the fire of youth and she would eventually tire of her passions, but Namatai was persistent.

Life in the village was straightforward and structured for the young girls. As soon as their breasts started showing, the girls would stop going to school and be married off to the older men who pounced on them like jackals on fresh meat. It was not uncommon for a man to claim to get visions from the gods showing him who they would court next and that is how most girls ended up with their life partners. The girls themselves did not mind. They would wait eagerly for the day they would finally cross the line into womanhood. It was every girl's dream to get married to the richer men of the village.

Namatai vowed she would never be like the other girls whose goals she believed were shallow. She had mapped out her future so well. She would go through high school and study Medicine at the University of Zimbabwe. No girl from the village had ever successfully made it past 'O' Level so the entire village kept its eyes on Namatai, anticipating failure. When she scooped five A's and a couple of B's, they all looked aside in shame. The same eyes followed her through her 'A' Levels and she still outdid herself and attained straight A's in Mathematics, Biology and Chemistry regardless of having missed some school days because of late payment of fees. Each time she was at school, she would borrow textbooks and take down the notes she had missed while she was barred from school.

The biggest conflict befell the Choto family when it was finally time for Namatai to go to university.

"Woman, why can't we be like other normal families and give our daughter away in marriage? SaGudza down there has shown some interest in the girl and he is a decent man. We should take advantage of this opportunity, not many men have cast their eyes on our daughter. SaGudza can give us a good bride price and he will support our family financially. We cannot send our daughter to study in the big city. There are predators there. She will get lost." It was Mr Choto pleading his case with his wife. "Where will we even get the money? What is so special about her?"

Mrs Choto stood her ground and vowed she would die first before fighting against her own daughter's goals. If it meant she had to starve, she would do it just to see her daughter's dreams through.

In the midst of the turmoil, Mrs Choto thought of her half-sister, Angela, whose husband was a lecturer at the University of Zimbabwe. She penned to her begging for help. After close to a month of anxious waiting, a response came back.

To Sandra Choto

Hello Sisi
It was nice to hear from you after such a long time.
I am happy to hear that Namatai is interested in pursuing her education at a higher level. I have always seen the fire in her and I know she will make a very good doctor. I only wish I had the same energy and passion when I was her age.
I spoke to my husband concerning Namatai's situation. David is a very strict man and he was unmoved at first. I finally managed to break through to him and he agreed to take Namatai in. We have an extra bedroom here that she can use. You only have to pay her tuition and we will cover the other costs.
Pass my warmest regards to the rest of the family.

Your loving sister
Angela

Mrs Choto read the letter twice before passing it to her husband who gave her curious glances from the other side of their small kitchen. Mr Choto read the letter; word by word with his finger tracing each line, his face stony and unmoving. When he was done reading it, he folded it neatly then took a deep breath before looking at his wife.

"I am not going to fight you anymore. I shall sell a cow and send the girl to university. When all of this backfires, don't say I didn't warn you."

Three weeks later, Namatai packed her bags and boarded a bus to Harare, leaving the village with mixed feelings. A few were proud of her, the first girl from the village to go to university, but a lot more despised her. Their general sentiment was that she thought herself more special than the other girls and people wanted to see where it would all end.

When Namatai got to Harare. Aunt Angela and Uncle David received her at the Mbare Musika Bus Terminus. She struggled to maintain a conversation with them because they both spoke English with a strange exotic accent. Aunt Angela would not stop asking questions about the village. She too had been born in the village but had escaped its claws of poverty when her mother separated from her father and left the village to find work in the city. That was perhaps the most rewarding misfortune of her life. Uncle David did not speak much. His forehead was constantly folded and his aura gave Namatai chills. By the time they got to their house on campus, Namatai had learnt she would have to speak less and listen more in order to enjoy her new life.

Namatai got her own room in the six-roomed house. Although it was modest by most standards, it was better than anything she had ever seen. There was a single bed by the window with floral curtains sweeping over it. There was a built-in wardrobe in a corner and a small desk and bookshelf next to it. Namatai could already envision herself drowning in books from that desk.

The first few days at the university were strange and draining. She looked on with disgust at the other girls who had brightly coloured hair and blouses that barely covered their stomachs. Back in the village, a woman was always supposed to be covered up as much as possible. It was taboo to see a woman's shoulders hanging out freely, worse still her thighs, but the girls at the university seemed not to care. The boys were even worse. Some plaited their hair and they sagged their pants. She wondered if the city had a way of corrupting people's minds to an extent where they acted like animals. Regardless of the craziness she saw around her; she would focus on her books, become a doctor and make enough money to take her family out of the village.

Namatai's routine was simple and constant. She woke up early to clean before anyone else was up. She would cook breakfast and then bath. As soon as the sun rose, she would set for the faculty library and study till it was time for lectures. She had no friends in class so she would sit alone in front. She was initially motivated to participate in discussions and ask questions. The mockery that however came her way because of her English accent which was apparently too rural and her unflattering outfits quickly drove her into a shell. She withdrew into her corner and shut herself away from everyone. The only thing that kept her going was her desire to excel academically and shame all those who looked down upon her.

Medical school was nothing like Namatai had imagined. Her life revolved around books and her schoolwork was always up to date, but she struggled to get anything higher than fifty-per cent in her in class tests. Each time she would re-evaluate her strategies and make adjustments which she thought would boost her grades, but her efforts proved futile.

It broke her heart. Her challenges in school were compounded by the fact that she did not have anyone to open up to. Aunt Angela spoke a little too much for Namatai's liking and so she never warmed up to her enough to talk about life matters. Uncle David was a non-starter; he was barely at home and when he was, he always seemed to be angry about something.

On one dreary morning, Namatai struggled more than usual to get out of bed. Her university experience was far from what she had imagined and she felt she had completely lost grip of her own life. The only thing that mattered to her was doing well in school but regardless of her efforts she was still underperforming. That morning, as she walked into class, she felt a crippling weight over her shoulders. She had been up all night, deep in thought and she could not get her mind to stop racing. She missed the village. She had always been an outcast but at least she had had peace of mind. Back in the village, she had no assignments, no deadlines to beat and best of all, she did not have to feel so poor. She suddenly felt her eyes watering and she walked to the back of the class where she sat hoping that no one would pay attention to her.

"Girl, are you alright?" a gentle voice spoke as a hand rested on Namatai's shoulder.

The words brought more tears to Namatai's eyes and she could not raise her head.

"Come on. Let's go outside," the voice whispered

Namatai did not resist. She knew if she stayed in the classroom, she was probably going to attract a lot more attention than she could handle. She felt the soft hand gripping her own as she walked out and she only looked at the face when they were outside. It was a familiar, welcoming face but she had never spoken to the girl before. She looked different, not like the girls that usually mocked her. She wore an off-white satin blouse that was neatly tucked into a pleated brown skirt. She had light brown locks that were slicked back into a bun. From her ears hung tiny pearl earrings. She smelled like clean linen. Namatai was all too busy scrutinising her when the girl spoke again.

"My name is Hannah. You are?"

"Namatai."

"You have such a beautiful name. Care to share what's going on?"

It was as if Namatai had been waiting for someone to ask that question. She had so much to say starting from the time when she was back in the village. The whole time Hannah listened attentively and nodded along. When Namatai was done pouring out her frustrations, Hannah finally spoke. "I am really sorry that you have had to deal with all that. I know exactly what you need."

Namatai's face brightened up.

"Come to my birthday party this weekend. You need to loosen up a bit."

Namatai shook her head. "I don't do parties."

"Come on. I will personally watch over you. It will be fun, trust me."

"And what will I tell my aunt?"

"Just tell her you have a group discussion for the next anatomy exam."

Namatai reluctantly took the advice. On the Friday evening, Hannah picked her up and they headed for Hatfield where the party would be held. By the time they reached the venue, a couple of their classmates and a lot more random youngsters were already littered around braai stands, plastic cups containing different shades of the liquid courage held casually in their hands. Shisha clouded the spot and joints were being passed around like baton sticks. Namatai could easily tell that most of the people present were not sober. She had never tasted alcohol or any drugs for that matter. The closest she had been to being high was the previous week when she had taken some Bioplus and three Red Bull energy drinks to stay awake while studying for her Physiology exam. She immediately felt like a lost sheep and receded into herself more than usual.

"Girl, you need to ease up," Hannah spoke as she handed her a plastic cup.

"I don't drink," Namatai said stiffly.

"Come on. This is not church. Just one drink. It will help you loosen up."

Namatai reluctantly took the tumbler. She grimaced as the bitter liquid flowed down her throat. After that first drink, it became easier to take another which was soon followed by another until she felt her head floating. The music vibrated in her veins and she soon found herself dancing along with the other wild youngsters. A joint was passed, and she puffed on it without giving it a second thought. She coughed and laughed hysterically before drowning herself in more beers.

The night went by fast and Namatai would not remember most of it. It was only in the morning that she found herself lying by the hedge in the backyard, shivering in the cold dew. She felt numb and her head throbbed. She remained on the ground for a couple of minutes and looked around. There were bottles everywhere and a few other people sat around smoking and drinking. About a metre away from her, she spotted her underwear and a chill immediately ran through her nerves. She stretched her legs and she felt something was different. A feeling of discomfort cocooned her from the waist going down. She stretched her hand and grabbed the underwear then slipped it into her pocket.

"Where is Hannah?" she asked around with tears in her eyes.

When she finally found Hannah sleeping comfortably in her bed, Namatai broke down in bitter tears. "You promised to look out for me. Why did you leave me in the hands of molesters?"

Hannah was barely awake as she spoke, "Molesters? Gosh Namatai. We were both so drunk. You made out with so many people last night, I could not stop you. You were literally begging for some action. You were out of control."

Those words broke Namatai's heart.

"At least tell me who did this to me," she burst out, holding out her faded underwear.

"Stop speaking like a victim Namatai. I don't know what you did or with who. Whatever the case it's not an excuse for being this dramatic. Now I have a very terrible headache and I need to sleep. I'll talk to you when you are calmer," Hannah said before covering her head to sleep.

Namatai was left in a prison of her own guilt. It made no sense that things could have gone so wrong in a space of a few hours. She could not stand herself and she regretted all the decisions that had led her up to this point. It made no sense that the one time she had decided to loosen up a bit, things had gone so terribly wrong. She was a good girl. She did not deserve this. She pondered on all this and she knew she would carry her story alone in her heart.

The days slowly went by but the weight in her chest would not dissipate. She felt herself drifting into depression.

The heat on the afternoon of the 16th of October was especially excruciating. The air was stagnant and a weight of humidity settled on the atmosphere, forcing everyone to remain indoors. Namatai was stuck in her room and strolled up and down in her light summer dress. She fanned herself with the hard cover of her old notebook. Her eyes were fixed on a bronze vase that decorated her room but her mind was very far from the present. The state of her health had been causing her a lot of worry. She had not felt like herself in a long time and it all traced back to the party.

Simple logic told her she was probably pregnant. In as much as she hated the possibility of it, it was only wise to find out the truth. Talk at school had said a mixture of urine and bleach would fizz and foam if one was pregnant and so she snuck to the kitchen while Aunt Angela slept off the heat and obtained her supplies. She cut an empty bottle of juice into half then urinated in it. She added a scoop of JIK bleach and watched for the next thirty minutes as nothing happened. Her relief was clouded by a lot of doubt. There really was no assurance that the test worked at all but at least the results gave her comfort for a while. She convinced herself to remain calm and face whatever was coming her way a day at a time.

The calm was only short lived as Namatai gradually felt some changes occurring within her. Her breasts were tender and nausea stuck around her on most mornings. She watched as she effortlessly gained weight, especially around her abdomen. After missing two periods she knew exactly what was going on and she had to act fast.

A suggestive thought lingered in her mind and as much as she hated the sound of it, it seemed the only reasonable thing to do. She had to get rid of the pregnancy without Aunt Angela ever finding out. She pondered on the idea for a couple of days before deciding to go forward and execute her plan.

Namatai woke up in the deep hours of the night, an ominous darkness shadowing everything. There had been a power cut and everything had gone silent. She reached under her pillow and grabbed a box of matches she had left there when she went to bed. She paused for a minute to calm her shaky breath then lit a matchstick. A candle stood next to her bed and she lit it. A dim light spread through the room. She walked over to the wall and took a metal hanger on which she always left her towel to dry. She straightened the hanger then took in deep breaths. Her rough idea of human anatomy told her that if she inserted the hanger deep enough into her vagina and to her uterus, she could scrape off an implanted zygote. She had heard through the grapevine that Nancy, a girl in her class had successfully done it.

Conflicting thoughts invaded Namatai's mind as she pulled off her underwear. There was a high chance she could pierce the wrong points and injure herself. There was a risk of haemorrhaging, and she could lose her life. She had heard of many girls who had lost their lives trying to abort at home. She was not ready to be a mother, but she definitely was not ready to die.

"A life without risks is the greatest risk of all," she thought to herself as she stretched her legs apart, clinging on to the drop of courage she had acquired from the nostalgic quote.

She grabbed the hanger with her right hand and pointed it upwards, between her legs. As soon as the cold metal touched her skin, she knew she was not going to go through with it. She threw the hanger away and burst into tears. She suppressed her cry and wished she had someone to talk to, someone with whom she could share everything that was going through her head. She wondered if there was even a single soul in the world who would listen to her story and not pin the blame on her.

"Oh God. Help me," she cried as she put her underwear back on and blew the candle out. She spent the rest of the night seated on the floor in the company of her deepest thoughts and the vague figures that danced in the darkness.

In the days that followed, her secret gradually swelled out of hiding.

"Damnit!" Namatai cursed at herself as she stared at her growing tummy in the mirror. It had been four months and she still had not notified Aunt Angela of what was going on. She still got up, cooked, cleaned and walked to school as if nothing was wrong. Her lousy grades which were now worse than before snitched that something was off.

Namatai used the African print wrapper she had received from her mother on her previous birthday and wound it tightly around her trunk until she could barely breathe and felt the discomfort in her abdomen. She concealed everything beneath her double-knit jersey and went to school. She knew it would only be so long until it began to raise questions and she almost expected it when it came.

Aunt Angela did not beat about the bush.

"Are you pregnant?"

"Ahh aunty, how can you ask me that?" Namatai could not think of a better response.

"You haven't answered my question. Are you or are you not pregnant?"

The question was followed by a dead silence that settled between them like an uninvited guest and Aunt Angela's tear-filled eyes remained fixed on Namatai. They were tears of anger.

"I am only going to ask you one last time; Are you pregnant?"

Namatai knew she was cornered. One way or the other, she was going to have to tell Aunt Angela the truth at some point. The words would not come out. She was filled with shame and guilt. She could only nod and cry.

"Unbelievable. Just unbelievable. I can't believe I took you out of the village for this."

"I am sorry. I did not mean for this to happen," Namatai cried.

"Are you trying to make my sister hate me? Do you even have any idea what my husband will do to me when he finds out?"

Namatai could not answer any of the questions that came her way. She too was struggling to make peace with everything that had happened to her.

"I am sending you back to the village," Aunt Angela spoke firmly.

"Aunty please. You can't do this to me. Please give me another chance."

Namatai's cries fell on deaf ears. A week later, she found herself back in the village, accompanied everywhere she went by eyes that dressed her down in disgust. They all held on to a single narrative, "Village girl who thought she was special shames her family." She wished they knew that beneath her thick skin was just another young girl, vulnerable and longing for a little understanding. After all, only she would carry the pain of her trauma in silence.

"Where is she? Where is that spoilt brat?"

"Calm down, Ba Tino. The child has been through enough already. Can we talk about this when you are a bit calm?" Mrs Choto tried to ease her husband's blazing rage, but her efforts only intensified the gravity of the situation.

"You see what I am talking about. You spoil this girl too much. Now look at the shame she has brought upon this family. I will only ask you one more time, where is the girl?"

"She is in her room. Crying. She has locked herself in there and she has been crying for hours."

"Crying? Pshh. Is she crying because she is pregnant or because she does not want to say who the father is? Huh?" The anger in his voice resurfaced with even greater force.

Mrs Choto stood in silence. She knew that nothing would ease her husband's anger. She wished she had the answers to her husband's questions, but she was as much in the dark as he was. She cursed herself for having pleaded with her husband to allow their daughter to go to university in the first place.

Then her husband shocked her, "How can this happen to a student of Medicine? A whole doctor. Tell her to pack up and we return to the university right now! No daughter of mine is going to give up that easily. She has to put up with my own sister in Zengeza this time as she has to finish that degree. No more games! That is the only way she will be able to look after the brat that she is carrying. O damn doctors of today!"

Friday the fourteenth

Everything about the morning was gloomy. Contrary to what the weather forecast had predicted, heavy clouds blanketed the skies and an unusual stillness ruled the atmosphere. The birds seemed to have gone silent and creation bowed down to an unsolicited murkiness. Richard held on tightly to his briefcase and took a deep breath before stepping off the doorstep.

"Best wishes daddy," his daughter's voice echoed from behind him and he turned to give a wave and a smile that struggled to mask his nervousness and fatigue.

Richard had not slept properly in four days. He had been at his desk trying to make sure he would be the most prepared interviewee. He was tired of being the reject, the "we enjoyed reading your application but..." This time, he would pay special attention to all the requirements and deliver exactly what was expected of him. He had to get this job and he was going to fight for it like his life depended on it because it did.

His life had veered from all his expectations and landed him in desperation. Richard had bagged several academic awards and graduated top of his class. Many people had predicted that he would be one of the most successful accountants in the country. Only two months after graduation, he had secured a contract as a trainee graduate at Banc ABC. Many people his age dreamt of working in a bank and yet he scooped the opportunity effortlessly. A year later, he married the love of his life, the beautiful Nandi and before Christmas they had welcomed a bouncing baby girl into the world. In those days, Richard rented an apartment in

Avondale and the site of his charcoal grey Toyota Rush SUV parked by the kitchen window announced his early success to the world.

And then his two-year contract ended and intraorganizational politics found Richard barred from getting a renewal. Allegations of him having assisted one of the top managers in embezzling funds popped up and the issue was to be dealt with without causing much drama. The proposal was to let Richard go quietly but much to his surprise, no other firm would hire him after that. Perhaps the secret had spread. Richard failed to get another job and from then everything on, went to waste. The first to go was the car. Eventually the rent was too high for their pockets and they moved to Richard's late parents' house. He cleared out a room for him and his family and left the others for the tenants. They joined the countless families that were stuck in the impoverished peri urban areas of Harare that were populated mostly by farm workers.

Over the next two years, Richard went to several interviews but he failed to secure a stable job. He occasionally got piece jobs that barely earned him enough to keep his family alive. Nandi had stepped in to help but she was gradually growing tired of living in a ghetto and selling vegetables. She had always been a city girl and came from a wealthy family and her patience was slowly running out. Her parents would remind her daily that she was welcome to return home any day but if she chose to stay with her broke man, they were not going to intervene.

Sharing a cottage with three other families was not the life Nandi had signed up for and only Richard's promises that he would make things right made her stay. She had threatened to leave him several times and she would not stop complaining. The Edgars interview invitation came at a time when he needed it the most. It rekindled his hope of being the man he wished to be, the man that could take care of his family.

As he walked down the path from his cottage, Richard went over a mental checklist of everything he needed for the interview. He quietly revised the answers he had prepared for some typical questions:

And why do you think we should hire you?

Over the past years I have acquired the relevant skills and experience which I believe will be of benefit to your company. I am fully aware of my capabilities and limitations and I always work with them in mind to produce the best results possible. Regardless of my current knowledge and skillset, I am always open to learn new things. I am willing to learn and adjust to the systems of your company so I can perform my duties to your satisfaction.

He smiled a bit as he went over his answers. If the roles were reversed, he would definitely hire himself. He was a perfect candidate for the job. He looked the part and he was confident about his qualifications.

At the bus stop, Richard tapped his foot impatiently and glanced at his watch twice each minute. He had left home three hours ahead of the interview time but after half an hour later, he was still standing by the roadside trying to flag down a lift. He watched as the clouds gradually became heavier and collided, creating chaos in the sky. A turbulence developed in the air and violent winds swept over the plane, carrying dust that landed on his thoroughly polished shoes and borrowed suit. Richard grew crescively anxious as the prospect of rain heightened. He kept his fingers crossed and hoped the skies would pity him and hold back the rains.

The first cold droplet that landed on his wrist was a sure sign that he was in trouble. Richard moved a little further into the gravel road and checked both sides but there was not a single vehicle in sight. The drop of rain was soon followed by others.

"Oh dammit," Richard cursed as the drops accumulated steadily into a heavy downpour. The closest shelter was at least a kilometre away and going back was not an option. He stood still in the rain, feeling it drench and penetrate his clothes. He held his briefcase tightly to his chest to try and keep it dry. The water rolled off the leather of the case and that gave him some comfort. In minutes, the rain had explored the entirety of his body and he stood shaking in the cold. As abruptly as they had started, the showers soon ceased and rays of sunshine graced the spot with sweet warmth.

Time was no longer on his side and Richard realised, in hindsight, that walking to town would have been a good idea. There was a chance that he could get transport down the road and it was better than standing and hoping someone would come to his rescue. He looked down at his scruffy, drenched suit and shook his head. No company would trust such a shabby man with their accounts. He still had to try though, for the sake of his family. He walked on; half of his confidence already stripped off. Had it not been for the "Men don't cry" gospel under which he had been raised, this was a moment he could have done with shedding a few tears.

A white car in the distance caught Richard's eye and his heart leaped. As he approached, however, he realised that it was not moving and his excitement died down.

What were the odds this car was going to town?

As he was about to inquire what the problem was, Richard saw the truck was stuck in mud. His first instinct was to mind his own business and walk right past, but his heart ached as he looked at the helpless driver, a greying man in an oversized Ankara shirt. He glanced at his watch again and realised he had only an hour left to get to town.

"Can I help, sir?"

The old man's face lit up. "Yes. Yes, my son. I have been stuck here for almost an hour now. I was hoping to stop other drivers and ask for assistance, but the road is dry today."

"I will try to push as you drive. Let's see if that works," Richard said as he placed his briefcase on the grass by the roadside.

Richard pulled up his sleeves and walked to the back of the truck. He gathered all his strength and pushed. He had hoped to quickly help the old man and be on his way, but he immediately realised he had grossly miscalculated. He pushed on still, without feeling any movement. As he tried to push harder, his feet slipped in the mud and he landed facedown, his white shirt getting an instant tint. The sound of his body landing dully on the ground pierced his heart. He felt the pain from his core; it was not physical. He felt cursed. It only made sense. Why else were these things happening to him? Why now?

Richard was still in the mud when the old man walked out and offered him a hand.

"I am so sorry, son." The man could see the tears that Richard was holding back and he wondered if the fall had really been that impactful.

"No sweat," Richard replied as he tried to no avail to clean himself up.

The old man watched helplessly as Richard cursed himself. He wished he had something better to offer him rather than words of sympathy. A tall, hefty man showed up on a motorbike together with a friend. He was an Agritex officer in the area and quickly identified the old man. He offered his help together with his friends. After a significant struggle, the truck was out of the mud and ready to hit the road.

"Thank you very much gentlemen. Get in my son; I will take you to town."

Richard was at this point conflicted. A part of him wanted to turn back and go home but a part of him still wanted to fight on. He was already running late. He quickly made up his mind; he would try his luck.

The first minutes of the journey were quieter than a monastic cell. Richard watched the trees race by as he reflected on his miserable life.

"Where are you going son? You seem very nervous," the old man asked.

"Job interview."

"Sure is one big interview I guess," the old man chuckled. "Are you sure that is all there is to it?"

Richard sighed and held his face wearily for a while before speaking. He felt the tears welling up again but as he had done his entire life, he pushed them back.

"I think I am cursed." His voice came out cracked. He cleared his throat before speaking again. "I think I am cursed. I have tried to do everything right, but I have lost everything. I am poor and broken and my wife is going to leave me soon if I do not get a breakthrough. I was hoping today would be my turn around but look at me now. I look pathetic. No one would hire me. I *am* pathetic. My life is meaningless. If Nandi leaves me, I am done for. I won't have anything to live for." Richard took a deep breath then continued. "I am oversharing. I am sorry."

"No, it's ok son. You really love her, right? Nandi?"

"More than anything else in the world"

"Do you think she loves you the same way?"

Richard pondered the question for some time. He remained quiet until the truck pulled over at a garage where the old man had said he would drop him off before he headed out of town in another direction.

As Richard walked out, the old man spoke, "It's ok to love and let go."

The words rung in his head and weighed on him. He stood and watched the truck drive away then remembered he was late for a job interview. He walked towards the Edgars shop which was about 10 minutes away from where he had been dropped off. As he turned a corner, his eye was caught by a young man, much like himself, dressed in a fine suit and walking out of the shop holding a briefcase. That is when it struck him. His briefcase! He began to shake with agitation. He could vividly visualise it resting by the roadside where he had placed it before helping the old man with his car. He wanted to slap himself and his stomach ached with regret. The interview invitation had stated that his certificates were a requirement for consideration for the post.

"I am done for," Richard whispered to himself as he finally gave in to the pressure he had been fighting the whole time and brushed off a tear from his left eye with the back of his hand.

He sat down on a slab facing the busy street and was lost in an eternity of passing bodies and cars. He reflected on his life and nothing made sense. He had moved from being an ambitious accountant to being the desperate guy whose world revolved around trying to make his wife love him and not leave. For the first time, he admitted to himself that he was unhappy. He had kept himself in a joyless corner, trying to prove he was worth something. It was time to liberate himself. He needed to rescue himself from the misery of being made to feel he was worthless. Yes, he was poor but he still deserved love and respect.

As he stood up, Richard forged some confidence and entered the shop. He had nothing else to lose. He walked to one of the counters and made his inquiry regarding the interview.

"Interview?" the lady behind the desk looked confused. She grabbed the landline to make a call.

"Interviews are going to be conducted tomorrow sir, Friday the fourteenth of May. I am afraid you are a day early."

More than stupid, he felt relieved as he walked out. He walked towards the taxi rank with a fresh burst of energy within him.

***

When he got home, it was around eight at night. Nandi's bags were packed. Basically, everything was packed. His clothes were piled in a corner waiting for him to share their disgrace.

"I have called my parents. They are on their way," she spoke firmly. Richard remained silent. He was not going to beg anymore. It was time to let go. He held on to his words and watched the unfolding of events.

When the Land Cruiser pulled up on their tiny yard, Richard watched from the window as Nandi carried her bags to the car. Her mother looked at him from outside with an eye that said, "you were never good enough for her." He was used to the disregard, so he did not flinch.

He hugged his daughter goodbye. It hurt him to have to be separated but he knew she was probably better off with her mother.

"I will come for my daughter." Those were his parting words.

In the cold of the night, Richard thought of every reason he had to continue living. Everything he stood for had slipped from his hands. Out of everything; his daughter was his main concern. Because of her; he convinced himself not to take his life that very night.

Before the break of dawn, Richard had bathed and he put on a clean set of formal clothes. He walked down the gravel road right ahead of the rising sun. He would not make the same mistake of waiting around for unreliable transport. Thirty minutes before the interview time, Richard found himself standing in front of the Edgars shop. He walked in and was directed to the waiting area.

When his name was finally called out, Richard walked confidently into the interview room but made sure to keep the expression of humility in his smile and the way he greeted everyone.

The interviewers were out for blood. They asked all the questions he had prepared for and more and at times, Richard would find himself stuttering. They neither smiled nor joked about anything. He still answered the questions to his best capacity.

Towards the end of the interview, the big question was finally asked, "Why do you think we should hire you?"

The paragraph he had rehearsed fled his mind and all that remained was the story inscribed on his heart.

He spoke slowly and gently, "I have lost everything. My life has changed drastically over the past months and only one thing has been constant, my love for accounting. When I was at my lowest, it is the only thing that made sense. I know that I was born for this. I am an accountant and I will perform my job whole heartedly. I may flatter you with how much of a good candidate I may be, but I am not going to do that. You should hire me because getting this job means the world to me. It is all that is left for me in this life."

An episode of silence followed his speech and the interviewers turned to their notepads and scribbled words he wished he could read. They did not give him even the slightest hint of reassurance. Richard left the room feeling he had messed up, but he also had a sense of liberation.

When he was finally called back and informed, he had got the job, Richard lost his breath for a minute. As they discussed the details of his contract, he felt an urge to hug everyone in his presence and share the joy he felt. He would be provided with accommodation in town and his transport and lunch costs would be covered. It was more than he could have asked for. He would be able to take care of his daughter.

Maybe he had been cursed before. Maybe Nandi was the curse. He laughed at his silly thoughts.

The Housekeeper

I had cleaned up after the Bushus for five years but on this freezing morning, the workload seemed more unbearable than usual. They had not added any extra tasks to the usual, but my spirits were so low even the energy within my muscle fibres had faltered. I brushed my feather broom over the surfaces; marble countertops, porcelain vases and granite sculptures, but I did not really pay attention to them like I normally did. I did not stop along the hallway to appreciate the oil paint portraits that lined the walls or to take a breath of the lavender plants that stood in a pot by the bathroom door. I even skipped a couple of rooms which I knew they would not notice and I swept dirt under their expensive, imported rugs. After the facade that was my cleaning, I headed to the kitchen for my tea break.

I was lost in thought when the kettle broke into a whistle. I poured myself a cup of tea and sat at the table, but my mind was still wrecked by chaos. I could not stop thinking of little Alice. Her fever had been worsening over the past few days and she was barely eating. She was vomiting daily. I had been loading her with paracetamol regardless of the doctors' recommendations. I could not gather enough money for the drugs and diagnostic tests they had prescribed. I was still two weeks away from my payday, so I had to find my own ways of making my daughter feel better.

I had already borrowed forty dollars from Mrs Bushu to pay school fees the previous week and she had been dismayed. She had given me the money with a heavy heart and lectured me for hours about how I needed to be clever with how I used my money. Mrs Bushu worked in finance and never missed an opportunity to talk about money. I had vowed to her that this would be the last time I would ask her for money, so I could not go back on my word. I needed to show her that I indeed listened when she spoke.

I had met Mrs Bushu on her way from work five years back. I had knocked frantically on the window of her Mercedes at a traffic stop. It was drizzling and I had Alice strapped to my back. She had opened the window begrudgingly and showed displeasure in how I was recklessly carrying my new-born out in the harsh weather. I explained how Alice had been born with a rare condition and needed surgery to save her life. I was just a single mother trying to make ends meet.

"And what is the name of this rare condition that your baby has?" she had asked.

I had not thought this through. The first word that came to my mind was asthma and I blurted it out with confidence.

"Asthma! My child has asthma. Please help us."

The traffic light turned green and Mrs Bushu drove into another street and parked by the roadside. I watched as she disembarked from the car and walked towards me. I walked right up to her with my hopes high.

She gave me an unsolicited lecture on how begging would not take me anywhere in life. She offered me a job as one of the labourers at her farm. I could not say no to the offer. I was not earning much as a beggar and I desperately needed money. I could not stop thanking her as she punched her cell number into my phone.

"By the way, asthma is not that rare and you do not need surgery for it. If you are gonna lie, at least be intelligent about it," she scoffed before turning her back on me.

I received the insult with a smile. I knew of a lot of people who were struggling to find employment and this was my jackpot.

I worked at the Bushu's farm for seven months until one day, Mrs Bushu showed up with a droopy face. She called me from the field and narrated how her maid had gone for the Easter holidays and not come back. She had also realised that a few of her clothes had gone missing and suspected they had been stolen. I sympathised with her.

"How do you feel about filling in for her while we look for someone more permanent?" Mrs Bushu had asked.

I did not need two minutes to make a decision. I worshipped Mrs Bushu and working in her house equated working in a palace.

In a few days I found myself working at the Bushu household in Greendale. I effortlessly got along with her children, and I knew she would never find a better helper than me.

I would soon realise that Mrs Bushu was so fond of me because she too had been in a similar position in the past. She had struggled with her first born as a single mother until she had met Mr Bushu, the man who helped turn her life around. I wished I could bump into my own Mr Bushu. I could not discredit the work that Mrs Bushu had put into making her dreams come true but had she not met her rich husband, she would not have been very far from where I was.

***

On this day, I decided I would go home early. I took out some beef from the freezer and put it in the sink to defrost then locked up as I had always done. I went over to the cottage where Takura, the gardener, stayed.

"*Hesi* babe," he greeted as he peeled a mango with a pocketknife.

I did not want to talk to him. After all, he was the reason I was in this financial dilemma. Takura had told me his mother had been diagnosed with breast cancer and needed chemotherapy. I had bought every last one of his words and loaned him half of my salary. He had promised to return it by the end of the week as soon as his diaspora brother had sent some money but all he had provided from then were excuses.

I did not respond to Takura's greeting. I only handed him the keys to the main house and walked away.

"Come on babe. Talk to me," his voice echoed from behind me, but I ignored him.

I took the path that led to the Kamfinsa Shopping Centre and hopped on a *kombi* to town. From there, I got another one to Kuwadzana where I stayed. I walked into Sisi Maggie's Pharmacy with the same sullen expression I had worn for the past week.

"Oh Maria dear, I cannot give you drugs on credit. Nothing has changed. I can't make any compromises on that," the till operator spoke before I even got to her.

I pulled out a crispy twenty dollar note and slapped it on the counter together with the crumbled up prescription.

"Oh! Where did you finally get this?"

I frowned and said nothing. I watched silently as she sorted out my order.

"Bad day huh?" she spoke again as she handed me the bag of pills.

I only nodded and walked out.

When I got home, Alice was coiled up in bed. I sat beside her and lay my hand on her forehead; her temperature was still so high. I had left her in the care of a fellow tenant but the house was empty, so it was likely that she had been stuck alone in this crowded room for hours. I was more disappointed than I was hurt. The pot of rice I had left in the morning was still untouched and an army of ants patrolled its edges like a bunch of junkies. A cockroach fell from the kitchen table and paced towards me. I aggressively squashed it beneath my slipper, allowing the pain I felt inside to gather in my foot.

"Wake up baby. *Mhamha* has brought you some medication to fix you up," I whispered in Alice's ear.

She twisted and turned before opening her eyes. They were bloodshot and narrower than usual.

"I am hungry, *mhamha*."

I immediately pulled out from my bag, a sandwich I had brought from the Bushus. She nibbled at the bread and soon said she felt nauseous. I popped the pills and handed them to her together with a bottle of water then put her back to sleep. I did not have it in me to prepare a proper meal or clean around like I normally did. I quickly slid into my nightdress and cupped myself close to Alice like a chicken brooding over her eggs. I listened carefully as her laboured breathing transformed into snores and I knew she was fast asleep.

I could not get myself to sleep. My eyes were fixed on the mini dressing table on the other side of the room, but I could barely see its components. Everything had gone grey, and my spirits were now lower than before. I had no one to call. There was no one to whom I could pour out everything that was haunting me. On days like this, I normally would have called Takura but I was mad at him. He even tried to call but

I did not pick up. He was the last person I wanted to entertain.

Before I knew it, it was morning. I lay my hand on Alice's forehead and her temperature was closer to normal. I tapped on her shoulder and she gave me a tiny smile that reassured me that she could get well after all. I leapt out of bed and rushed to the kitchen with a smile. It was almost as if I had immediately been freed from the demons that had kept me up the whole night.

I cleaned up the room and prepared enough food to take Alice through the day. If I had any other option, I would not leave her under the supervision of my irresponsible fellow tenants, but they were the closest thing I had to family. Because of work, I had not managed to make a lot of friends in the area. I cleaned myself up and made sure Alice had bathed before I left for work.

I arrived in Greendale a little late but I was unbothered. By the time I normally got to work, the Bushus would have already left and I would always collect the keys from Takura. When I got to the gate, I was surprised to find the sprinklers turned off. Takura would always water the lawn first thing in the morning. I slid the gate open and the second weird thing I saw was Mrs Bushu's car still parked in the driveway. I walked straight to the kitchen door and knocked gently. The door swung open in seconds and Mrs Bushu looked at me with a foreign expression that instantly sent a shiver to my shoulder blades.

"You're late," she charged at me as she walked back to the kitchen counter and grabbed her cup of coffee.

"I am sorry ma'am," I replied with my face down as I quickly pulled out my apron from my handbag.

"That is the problem with you people."

"I am sorry ma'am."

"You can't be helped."

"I am sorry ma'am."

"Will you shut up, please. Just shut up and listen to what I have to say. And look at me when I speak to you, will ya?"

I froze and faced her. She looked like an animal. I quickly realised that this was not only about me being late for work.

"I fired Takura."

My heart cracked at her words and for a second, I felt all the hairs on my body stretch out and fall back again.

"Three years! I stayed with Takura for three years. I treated him like family. I took great care of that boy and his poor family. And after all that he still decides to steal from me. I have always forgiven his shortcomings, but theft is an extreme. Who knows what else he stole? Huh? Who knows what else he was up to here? Were you also part of his shenanigans?"

I shook my head.

"That bastard is lucky. I should have called the police on him. He would get a proper beating and learn not to steal again."

There was silence for a while. I was not sure if I was allowed to speak yet.

Hesitantly, I asked, "What did he steal?"

"Twenty dollars. That's how I knew it was him. He asked me for twenty dollars yesterday and I told him to wait for his salary. I kept thinking about it and eventually felt bad. I had actually decided I would give him the money after work. It so happened that I forgot my wallet here. I did not think he would go to the lengths of stealing the money from me."

"I am sorry ma'am," I whispered.

"I have to head to work now. I am behind time. This better be the last time you show up here late."

"Ok ma'am."

"Now go about your work and do it properly. Let it be known that there will be no place for thieves in this house."

I nodded and finally gave a sigh of relief when Mrs Bushu left the house.

As soon as the gate closed behind her, I grabbed my phone and dialled Takura's number. The first two times, he ended the calls but I called again. He picked the third.

"I told you not to call when my wife is around. What do you want?" His voice was hushed but the anger was clear.

"Oh I am sorry, Takura. I heard about what happened and I just had to check on you."

"Why are you sorry? Is it because you stole that money and now you just want to clear your conscience?"

"Ah Taku. How can you make such strong accusations?"

"Tell me I am wrong then."

He was right. I had found Mrs Bushu's wallet in the dining room. I had only slipped out twenty dollars. I needed to save my child. It was only twenty dollars, the same amount she claimed she gave to her children for snacks each day. I did not think she would even notice. Why did she even care about twenty dollars when she had piles of money? I had slipped the note into my apron and placed the wallet back where I had found it.

"I'm sorry, Takura. My daughter was really sick. I did what I had to do. I did not think she would make a fuss about it."

"This whole time I have been trying to convince myself that this has been one big misunderstanding and that the money was never stolen in the first place. You were of course my suspect but I hoped I would be wrong. You have to confess."

"I cannot do that. I cannot lose this job. It's all I have. How will I take care of my daughter?"

"You should have thought about that before you stole from your employer. She said she trusted you and that you would never steal from her. She trusted you over me. Now do the honourable thing. Come clean."

"I know I messed up Takura, but you need to help me out here. You have connections. You can easily get another job. If I lose this one, I will be in trouble. Please help me out, babe."

"Don't babe me. As far as I am concerned, our little situationship is over. I am making amends with my wife. Now I am giving you a chance to confess or I will do it for you."

"If you sell me out, I will tell your wife about our little situationship then," I firmly blurted the words out and hung up. I was not sure if my threat was good enough to keep Takura silent. I dropped my phone and helplessly sat on the floor.

Prayer Mountain

For a good thirty-minutes, I sat behind the library and stared at my report card as if the D's and E's would shy away and miraculously turn into A's. I could already feel my buttocks twitching just by imagining how badly Baba had whipped me the previous academic term for only getting a single A and a chain of C's. I had not been able to sit or walk properly for an entire week. With my current results, Baba would murder me.

I pulled out the tiny bottle of ink eraser gel I had stolen from Mr Ndlovu's office. I took my time to carefully turn my D's into A's and E's into B's. I looked at the page for five minutes while trying hard to convince myself no one would notice what I had done. I rolled the report card and shoved it into my bag then headed home.

There was something ritualistic about the last day of school at Gwindingwi High. This was the only day when both teachers and students interacted in good cheer with the prospects of restful holidays.

"Goodbye *ma*teacher, *toenda kunozorora*," the entire school would sing and dance as a way of bidding farewell to the teachers. The junior students would give out a marvellous soprano melody while the seniors added bass to the song.

It seemed I was the only one who never shared in the joy of the last day of school. I was still in Form 2 but could not wait to be done with high school for good.

Unlike the other students, I dreaded the holidays. My routine had become so monotonous. I would always be the last to leave school while reflecting on what it is that I really needed to do in order to pass like the other students. I knew the greater part of my holiday would quickly rush by as I endured the consequences of having poor grades. I always received a remarkable whooping that made me swear I would never fail again then a huge load of manual labour would be dumped on me.

"This ought to teach you to work hard in school," Amai would always snarl at me each time she spotted even the tiniest drop of tears peeping from my eyes.

I always preferred it when Amai got to me before Baba did. Her beating was a little more bearable. She always used a belt and she would not stop until she could no longer breathe properly. She would shout all sorts of insults in between swings of the belt and that dissipated her energy. The case was different with Baba. He would always pick five thick sticks from the mulberry tree. I had never understood his obsession with the number five. He owned five goats; smoked five cigarettes each day and would only sleep for five hours. Maybe his rumoured girlfriend had been born on the fifth. Baba did not care if you were a girl or a boy. He would expose your buttocks and hit them so hard until each stick broke. I always got chills all over my body each time I pictured his beating.

Mukoma Tawa had been Baba's last victim. Reports had got to Baba that he had been skipping school and drinking cheap beer with some school dropouts at the local shopping centre. Despite being so muscular and tough, Mukoma Tawa had cried out so loud till he vomited all the beer he had drunk.

I arrived home just around midday. I had hoped Baba would be at work but when I saw his bicycle parked under the mulberry tree, I knew he was home early. Little Chipo was playing *nhodo* with her friends close to the veranda, so I walked up to them first.

"Is Amai around?" I asked in a hushed voice.

"No. She has gone to the prayer mountain," Chipo answered without looking at me.

"Stupid prayer mountain," I cursed silently. I never knew where it was, but every week Amai would fast and go to the prayer mountain. I hated how she was so convinced that our family was bewitched and needed serious prayers to lift the curse. She said that is why Baba never got a promotion at work, why Mukoma Tawa acted like a loser, why I was a sworn dunderhead in school and why Chipo had been born with deformed feet. I only hated one thing more than the prayer mountain; that stupid Prophet Demojena. He was the one who filled Amai's head with that witchcraft nonsense.

I frowned and walked into our sitting room. Baba was perched on his favourite sofa and had a cigarette balanced between his lips. The smoke made the room a little hazy. I did not mind the smell; I had grown accustomed to it. The sun peeped through the holes of the closed curtains, giving an orange tint to the uncomfortably hot room. Baba's eyes were fixed on the previous day's Manica Post newspaper. I had heard rumours that he had not made it past the fourth grade and it only made sense seeing how he took hours on each page. He would read the same newspaper all week until he got another copy. I never dared to ask him about it. He did not like it when people undermined his competence.

"*Masikati* Baba," I greeted as I walked to the sofa opposite to him. I folded myself up and waited with bated breath for him to ask for the report card.

"Good afternoon my daughter. Did you pass?"

I silently nodded and handed him the tattered booklet.

He flipped through the pages, scanning each and every one of them before settling on the most recent one. For the minutes that followed, I waited silently for his comments.

"Five A's and three B's hmmm. What an improvement!" he eventually said and my face lit up.

"I tried my best Baba," I replied.

"Well done my daughter. Go and get changed. I will take you to the grocery store and buy you whatever you want."

"Thank you, Baba!" I leapt in joy to the room I shared with my little sister.

I could not contain my excitement. For the first time in ages, I would not get a disabling whooping. Why had I not thought of this before?

I knelt on the gritty floor and quickly pulled out my suitcase which stayed under the bed. I threw it on the bed then flipped it open. My favourite 'Teenage Mutant Ninja Turtles' t-shirt was right on top. I grabbed it together with a pair of jeans. It was a bit torn and starting to fade but I still loved the army green. Amai had got it from a thrift shop the last time she had visited Harare. I stretched my hand to my back then unzipped my school dress. I allowed it to fall freely to my feet. Before I could move another inch, the door opened behind me. My first instinct was to pick my dress and cover myself up but I was forced to stop midway when the sound of thunder robbed the room and the worst pain grabbed my back. When the second strike landed, I knew exactly what was happening.

"So, you think you are clever huh?" Baba bellowed as he drew me closer to him for another strike. He shoved my head in between his thighs and locked me in before attacking my naked buttocks.

"You thought I wouldn't see the alterations you made to your results huh. An A in Maths but the comment says 'Work hard.' You honestly think I am that gullible. You think I am that stupid? So you listen to those rumours that say your father is dull, huh?" Baba kept shouting as heavy lashes rained on me. His voice was soon drowned in my cries as I begged for forgiveness, but he would not stop. The first stick broke and he picked another and another. I cried until I could no longer do so and when he was finally done with me, he let me fall to the ground like a rotten fruit.

I remained on the same spot for minutes, contemplating on the ugliness of my own life. I could not believe he was my own father. What father would do that to his own child?

I looked at my cool t-shirt that now lay crumpled up on the floor and it seemed to mock me. I picked myself up and shoved it back into the bag then gingerly put on a loose dress. Intense pain radiated from behind me each time I moved a muscle.

Hatred welled up within me and I dreaded leaving the room. I did not have it in me to face my father. He was a monster.

After close to an hour, I silently walked out of the room. Baba was back on his sofa, smoking. I kept my gaze as far from him as possible as I left the house. I walked to the back of the house where he kept a trunk of junk that seemed to have anything you could ever think of. I opened it and scrambled through it till I found a rope. I quickly shoved it into my pocket then walked towards the woods.

The thought on my mind was to take my life so Baba would have to live with the guilt of having beaten me to my grave. I soon discarded that idea as I realised, I did not want to hurt myself. I would disappear instead; stay in the woods for the night and give him a scare. I would find myself a place to stay for the night then return home the next day.

I looked at the trees around me and they were either dried up or getting there. I kept walking and looking around. I at least deserved to stay in an aesthetically pleasing place. As I walked on, the terrain changed. Scattered boulders and balancing rocks decorated the space. I noticed the grass becoming progressively greener till I reached a stream. The water flowed peacefully past carved rocks and little birds came for a drink. This was it, the perfect spot.

I spotted a Muzhanje tree close by. I climbed the tree then balanced myself between two branches. I drew out the rope and stared at it for minutes. I had seen a lady securing herself with a rope on trees and sleeping there on television. I was going to do the same. All I had to do was figure out how exactly I would secure the knots. As I planned my adventure, a weird sound grabbed my attention and I froze.

I listened quietly and the sound came again. At first, it sounded like suppressed laughter then it seemed like moans. My inquisitive mind could not let it get past me. I climbed down the tree and slowly crawled towards the strange noise.

The noise became progressively louder, and as I got closer, I could make out a female voice and a male voice. The female voice giggled.

I knelt behind a rock and craned my neck to try and see what was happening, but the long brown grass obstructed my view. A vague outline of what seemed like an intimate moment is all I could see. I tried to move the grass for a clearer view and accidentally snapped a twig.

"Who is there?" the male voice charged and there was silence. "Show yourself Satan," the voice came again and a rock landed right next to me.

I slowly picked myself up with my face cast down in shame. I was not ready to look at them.

"Ahh, Ruvimbo!" Amai exclaimed as she pulled down her dress and fixed her bra. I was more confused than she was. "What are you doing here Ruvimbo? Who brought you here?" She had many questions but I gave no answers.

I looked at Prophet Demojena and his belt was undone. He looked uglier than ever and the sweat on his face glistened in the sun. I figured I hated him more than Baba.

"Are you also here for prayers?" he asked and I frowned.

I turned my gaze to Amai who was all of a sudden praying in tongues.

"So, this is Prayer Mountain?"

She did not look at me. A devious smile settled on my face. I now had the perfect revenge for Baba. This news would destroy him.

About the author

Nyasha Melissa Chiyanike is a young Zimbabwean writer who has a passion for storytelling and youth empowerment. She is a medical student at the University of Zimbabwe where she balances her academic pursuits and creative endeavours. She contributed to the Turquoise Dreams short story anthology in 2020 which showcased the voices of emerging Zimbabwean women writers. This is her first publication alone.

Nyasha believes that writing is a powerful tool for change and empowerment, and she encourages other young people to pursue their dreams and express themselves through words. She looks forward to sharing more of her stories with the world.

9 781914 287534